The Dominion of Signs

The Dominion of Signs

Television, Advertising, and Other New Zealand Fictions

Nick Perry

AUCKLAND UNIVERSITY PRESS

First published 1994
Auckland University Press
University of Auckland
Private Bag 92019, Auckland
New Zealand

ISBN 1 86940 100 X

Publication is assisted by the Literature Programme, Queen Elizabeth II Arts Council

Printed in Wellington by GP Print Ltd

Distributed outside New Zealand by Oxford University Press

For Kate and Lisa

Contents

Acknowledgements

There is a tendency for the author's partner to get relegated to a position of 'last but not least', providing tea, sympathy and keeping the kids out of the way. Jan's contribution to this book goes beyond our shared addiction to the pleasures of coffee, criticism and wondering what our girls are up to. As an American for whom Mark Twain and Maya Angelou are part of a single tradition, she has spent more than twenty years persuading me of the deep continuities between affection and intelligence. I hope some of that lesson shows through.

The lesson I learned from an old friend and ex-colleague Roy Wilkie also began more than twenty years ago. At that time the (British) universities viewed popular culture with disdain and treated it with contempt. Yet Roy combined the analytic skills of a philosophical training with ardent support for Glasgow Celtic, jazz connoisseurship, a taste for science fiction and an enthusiasm for Z Cars. By his way of living it, he first suggested to me what a defence in depth of popular culture might actually look like.

AUP's Elizabeth Caffin, as befits the ideal editor, chose the ideal reader for the draft manuscript—one responsive to its general intent, perceptive on its limitations, and innovative on how those limitations might be minimised and that intent might better be realised. I have also been influenced by conversations with, or correspondence from, or comments by Ian Carter, John Deeks, Geoff Fougere, Roger Horrocks, Geoff Lealand, Bob Lingard and Ann Poulsen. Roger Horrocks was also very helpful in obtaining video graphic prints. Thanks to Metro magazine for granting permission to reproduce a double page spread from their June 1988 issue, and to Toyota New Zealand and the BBQ Factory for the use of images from their commercials. Every effort was made to obtain consent for the use of the images and illustrations featured in this book, but replies were not always received.

I would also like to thank Kate and Lisa for reasons which should be evident in Chapter One, and Mr R. G. Kitchen and Mr C. R. Smaill for reasons which are made clear in the book's closing pages.

Gaynor van Beurden converted the text into WordPerfect and continued to tolerate my anachronistic allegiance to a word processing program that is almost as ancient as our family car.

Preface

Chapter Two has its origins in 'Common Coinage: Telethon and Cultural Criticism in New Zealand', *Landfall*, 149, 1984, pp.89-103, and 'Channel Vision', the opening lecture in the Auckland University 1987 Winter Lecture Series, 'The Mass Media: Threats and Opportunities', convened by Roger Horrocks. The present version is a revised and extended version of 'Cinderella and the Silver Mercedes' as published in David Novitz and W. E. Wilmott (eds.), *Culture and Identity in New Zealand*, (1989) Wellington, Government Print. The initial version of Chapter Three was a response to a request to write 'something on New Zealand' for the Japanese Popular Culture Association and was subsequently presented at a conference on 'Post Colonial Formations and Cultural Policy' at Griffith University, Queensland, in July 1993. Chapter Four is based on a presidential address to the Annual Conference of the Sociological Association of Australia and New Zealand at the University of New England, Armidale, N.S.W., July 1986. It subsequently appeared under the present title in *Landfall*, 164, 1987, pp.462-73. A version of Chapter Five was published in *Sites*, 21, 1990, pp.113-27. Chapter Six made its first appearance in *Antic*, 4, 1988, pp.109-18. Under the title of 'Peripheral Visions', an early version of Chapter Seven was part of a seminar series at the Stout Research Centre, Victoria University of Wellington, in June, 1985. It was subsequently published under the title it has in this book in *Islands*, 38, 1987, pp.161-77. In its present form it also includes material from the previously mentioned 1984 *Landfall* essay. Chapter Eight draws on two essays: '"Being There", Being Here and *Being Pakeha*' in *Sites*, 13, 1987, pp.32-36, together with a review of *Theory K* published in the *Listener* of 13 June 1987. The latter appeared under the heading 'In Pursuit of Excellence' but was submitted as 'From Breathless to Deathless'. My thanks for permission to use the material in this book.

ONE

Introduction

Does the Book Stop Here?

We have two teenage daughters, a rabbit hutch, about 2000 books, and a ten-year-old Honda Civic (we lost the rabbit and sold the BMW). The books, car and hutch add an idiosyncratic flavour to that otherwise generic mixture of embarrassment and affection with which offspring view their parents. Our no-longer-children children see this particular combination of icons and their owners as not-quite-relics; as outmoded but not yet usurped. They recognise that at times the elements of this assemblage can and do still function, have value, are even necessary. The tone of this acknowledgement is, however, not matter of fact (or grudging or generous, for that matter). It is instead exasperated *and* charitable *and* sardonic, and all of these at once.

This mobile and plural response to a more obviously archival form of life does not just signal the practice of lives being formed. It also measures the distance between a literary-based version of what culture might mean and the present state-of-the-art amongst our daughters and their friends. For them, the literary in its various forms is understood as incidental tributaries of the main channel. Yet they all began to read before they were a year old. Not books, of course, but rather the intimate pattern of parental gesture and expression, the markers and entrances to the storehouses of language and speech, the cultural distribution of furniture within a room. And of course television. An enduring and still vivid memory that I have of our first-born's first year was of entering the lounge one day and seeing her sitting on the floor with her back towards me, cross-legged, straight-backed, fully absorbed and attentive as the commercials made their familiar pitch on the small screen. In my mind, then as now, this common-enough representation of domestic life spontaneously and instantaneously interlocks and overlaps with another image. It comes from a news photograph taken during the campus struggles of the sixties. In the left-of-centre foreground a single, vulnerable figure sits, back to camera, cross-legged, straight-backed but loose-limbed, and facing a uniform and anonymous phalanx of helmets, riot-shields and guns. They fill the middle ground and are advancing slowly towards the figure, the photographer and by implication the person viewing the picture.

This says nothing about the actual relation between small children and television, as it has been explored by, for example, such researchers as Hodge and Tripp (1986). But in as much as this kind of reaction is prompted by the impulse to construct a protective magic circle around whatever matters to us, it does speak directly, if idiosyncratically, to many of those real anxieties and surreal fantasies to which television continuously gives rise. At a time when our indifference to one another is both officially approved and carefully nurtured, such responses are cultural markers of some consequence; a licence to control at their myopic worst but a kind of loving at their more open best.

This poses a double problem; how to resist the control and how to rescue the openness. By focusing on the first, it is possible to make a modest contribution to the second. For example, in 1989 Roger Horrocks first succeeded in convening an undergraduate course on film and television at the University of Auckland. Entry into this second-year paper was, and is, highly restricted and very competitive, recruiting from among the best and brightest students in the Arts faculty. Yet what emerged again and again from the first tutorials was the extent to which their interest in film and (especially) television had been the subject of parental controls and educational opprobrium. Such interest was seen as not merely incidental to real learning but as actively opposed to it. There was an antipathy to the media both as a subject of enthusiasm and as an object of study for those who are academically able. *They* could do better.

This notion of a split between students' own day-to-day cultural preoccupations and the received conception of education is neither new nor news. Teachers and educators have long been attuned to such a division and have long sought to bridge it. But youth culture and the mass media now reach right across the very distinctions and discriminations to which a traditional liberal education is dedicated. They encroach upon its most basic assumptions. However ingenious or ingenuous the use of them as teaching aids in the service of the received pattern may be, the media are much more than instruments through which learning may be extended. The medium may not (yet) be the message, but it *is* the measure, both setting the benchmarks for day-to-day cultural judgements and social evaluation, and providing the symbolic currency which allows such trans-actions to take place. As the common coinage of contemporary culture, the media are the pervasive, taken-for-granted environment in which learning now occurs.

Thus our daughters' typical cultural work in progress consists of a supple and discriminating enthusiasm for specific thrash/grunge bands, soft toys, Doc Marten boots, silk pyjamas, *Ren and Stimpy*, dad's shirts, BFM radio, *Dolly* magazine and touch rugby. Although the content of such combinations may vary, this particular grouping is recognisably a proxy for the general pattern of preferences amongst adolescents and post-adolescents. A point to note is that the constituent elements of this *lingua franca* are made to (imperfectly) cohere, and seen to make sense, in ways that an exacting and difficult writer like Jorge Luis Borges might envy. Yet the producers of popular programmes and magazines take all of this ordered and organised fragmentation for granted. Characteristically, they also deny being tantamount to perpetrators of The Flood (as their critics insist). They argue instead that popular taste is simply the sea in which they swim and that contemporary youth culture is merely its latest wave.

Academic traditionalists (of both the left and the right) are, by con-trast, left high and dry. What these protagonists share is an aversion to the popular currents which swirl around it and them. Their own pickings are, however, getting thinner and there is a manifest edginess to those struggles amongst themselves over possession of that (once) firm cultural ground which remains. Those brief but intense flurries of misanthropic fury which sometimes accompany their critical descent upon each other's work might be said to signal this larger problem. But at their learned and brilliant best, as, for example, in George Steiner's *In Bluebeard's Castle* (1971) and *On Difficulty and Other Essays* (1978), they easily shrug off all attempts at easy definition. The erosion of Steiner's favoured terrain induces a prose which both transparently foregrounds and effectively transcends its own ideological provenance. He persistently thinks for-ward, but to a future which is understood as limited and diminished; the pervasive mood wavers between a wholly unsentimental nostalgia and a clear-eyed melancholy. Steiner provides both a lucid summation of the institutional preconditions and implicit power relations which sustained the primacy of 'the book' and a sublime testament to its lost authority, a loss for which his texts themselves provide a consolation and a legacy.

By comparison, works like Allan Bloom's *The Closing of the American Mind* (1987) and E. D. Hirsch's *Cultural Literacy* (1987) seem mordant and nervy in tone, evidence of a near panic of which the very excesses helped secure their (commercial, upmarket) successes. There is something endearingly loopy about Bloom's (1987, pp.74-81) apocalyptic account of rock music in general, and Mick Jagger in particular, even though (or perhaps because) it has been made familiar by the antipathetic images of US high-school principals which emanate from the studios of Hollywood and Burbank. His interpretation is filtered through Nietzsche and sanctioned by Plato, but the basic premiss is the presence of folk devils and the controlling sentiments are fear and loathing. In like fashion, Bloom approaches Woody Allen's *Zelig* through Heidegger and finds it badly wanting, and 'never nearly as funny as was Kafka' (1987, p.146). There is no sense that the film might be of philosophical (or pedagogical, or artistic, or commercial) interest because of its attempt to use and extend a popular medium in a distinctively *cinematic* way. The problem is not that Allan Bloom seems ignorant of (Woody Allen's commanding knowledge of) the language of film or (Mick Jagger's modestly talented dependence upon) the tradition of the blues. The problem is his conviction that such ignorance does not matter, that it does not materially affect either his ability to pass such judgements or their quality. In this sense what Bloom has to say about his students' exasperation with Plato provides a roundly rhetorical and ironic commentary on the limitations of his own stance:

> The very fact of their fury shows how much Plato threatens what is dear and intimate to them . . . Yet if a student can—and this is most difficult and unusual—draw back, get a critical distance on what he clings to, come to doubt the ultimate value of what he loves, he has taken the first and most difficult step towards the philosophic conversion. Indignation is the soul's defense against the wound of doubt about its own; it reorders the cosmos to support the justice of its cause . . . Recognising indignation for what it is constitutes knowledge of the soul. (Bloom 1987, p.71)

The dilemma for authors like Bloom and Hirsch is that while their conception of what education means debars them from avoiding popular culture, it also debars them from understanding it. This situation is widely enough distributed for their texts to have become a small part of the very cultural phenomenon that they are concerned to deprecate, a ripple at its edges.[1] They do not make waves. In fact, the main narrative lines of such critiques have been so familiar for so long as to be routinely employed by the (purportedly irredeemable) culture industries themselves (examples which come to mind are *The Running Man, Brazil, Network, Broadcast News, Bladerunner,* even *Robocop*). Umberto Eco has not only sardonically and self-mockingly charted the typical trajectory of such traditional critical responses. He has also wryly exposed the grim fairy tale which sustains them:

> Once upon a time there were the mass media and they were wicked, of course, and there was a guilty party. Then there were the virtuous voices that accused the criminals. And Art (ah, what luck) offered alternatives for those who were not prisoners of the mass media.
> Well, it's all over. We have to start again from the beginning, asking one another what's going on. (Eco 1987, p.150)

Eco's words are best understood as a subversion of traditional orthodoxies and a commitment to greater methodological humility. They are *not* a ratification of the principle that 'anything goes'. Such openness towards the popular is a methodological tactic, not an epistemological commitment; popular sentiment is not assumed to enjoy a privileged position in relationship to truth, or taste, or progress. But that Eco's remarks might admit of such an interpretation does point to a continuing difficulty which besets those academic approaches which are more directly populist than his. Because the impulses which inform and sustain such works are characteristically democratic, the notion of a transcendent cultural standard is typically repudiated in favour of ethnographic inquiry and/or allowing popular texts to play. But in their concern to distance themselves from moribund versions of tradition, the tendency has been for such authors to canonise not just their own constructions of popular sentiments but to tacitly ratify the social arrangements which sustain them. In effect, there is a drift away from the conception of a democratic culture as an aspiration and towards seeing it as an accomplishment.

In the United States such 'academic populism' is perhaps most closely identified with the American Popular Culture Association and the *Journal of Popular Culture*. It received a specifically local inflection in New Zealand through the work of Geoff Lealand (1988). In Australia during the 1980s it was channelled through marxism, as in the long-running but inconclusive debate in the journal *Arena* involving John Docker and others. Both the range and quality of Australian contributions have developed rapidly. More recent studies, such as the excursions to the beach by Fiske *et al.* in *Myths of Oz* (1987) or his solo browsings in shopping malls and television quiz shows (Fiske 1989a; 1989b), are distinguished by a layered, more ambivalent and questioning version of populism. This seems to be at once distinctively Australian and a beneficiary of the contrast between British and American approaches (the British-born Fiske now teaches in the United States).

With varying degrees of sophistication these studies exemplify Raymond Williams's maxim that 'culture is ordinary', and this is both their strength and their weakness. The strength is that academic populism constitutes a reminder and a provocation, a challenging of critical and cultural hierarchies through the display of textual or ethnographic complexity in the everyday realm. The weakness is that the predisposition towards respect for popular judgements may lapse into what a Glaswegian colleague of mine once called the 'prolier than thou' syndrome, whether in its culture-by-numbers empiricist version or as a permutation on socialist realism. Such responses have, however, progressively given way to a recognition that 'the popular' is itself contested, and that popularity is in no way inconsistent with divided and perhaps divisive patterns of response. 'Whose popular culture?' and 'popular with whom?' are questions which now persistently insinuate themselves. The rather different problem of too much sophistication derives, in part, from such enhanced awareness. Such studies may still fly under the flag of populism but the celebration of popular culture becomes displaced by its cerebration. The initial focus of enquiry gives way to an emphasis on the development of theory *per se* and with it a consolidation of the role of active, knowing and ingenious constructors of what ordinary (i.e. *other* people's) culture might mean (cf. Morris 1990). One kind of culture is, in effect, transcribed through the assumptions and into the categories which are characteristic of another. What can too easily get lost in such translation is what is specifically 'cultural' about popular culture, that which Robert Warshow (1961) called 'the immediate experience'.

There are, however, some populist studies which are both exempt from such objections and profoundly at one with the milieu which is their subject matter. For example, just as Steiner's requiem for tradition succeeds in making that tradition live, so too does a fine work such as Greil Marcus's (1975) risky, generous, emotionally charged, want-it-all book on rock 'n' roll break through the limits of populism onto a terrain hitherto only glimpsed. Marcus's text effectively invents an imaginary space where Elvis and Herman Melville, Randy Newman and D. H. Lawrence, James Agee and other co-conspirators might not just meet, but recognise the other(s). What results is a narrative which keeps faith both with a populist heritage and its musical representation, and with a sophisticated literary culture through which its author's passions are not so much refined as distilled. It is entirely plausible that Eco would read Marcus with the pleasure of recognising a wayward but kindred spirit. It is possible, but less certain, that Steiner would do the same—it would, after all, require granting absolution to an author who confesses to having written a banned rock 'n' roll song called 'I Can't Get No Nookie'. Bloom, of course, would get no satisfaction from the book at all. But what is most telling is the comment on his now classic text which Marcus himself most values. It came from a University of Alabama professor who refused to believe that 'a Yankee' could have written it. The lines of Harvard, Princeton and Chicago intellectuals that parade approvingly across the dust jacket of Bloom's book seem parochial by comparison. It is, finally, not Bloom but Marcus who has a secure lien on the American meaning of soul.

What Eco, Steiner and Marcus have in their different ways recognised is the failure of a particular critical conceit, not the end of criticism as such. That the extant critical assumptions and principles developed and refined in relation to literacy and the book are not universal is, of course, now part of a widening critique mounted from within the humanities both by home-grown subversives and by the hitherto marginal or excluded. The conceit that is here in question, however, is not just that privileging of particular practitioners, texts and practices through which the idea of a canon is constructed and institutionalised. Rather it is the privileging of so distinctive and specific a technology of representation as literary practice as the basis for critical evaluation in general. The very idea that such procedural assumptions could not only migrate from their original location to others, but could also enforce their authority over the new territories, depended upon the expansion of an empire, the empire of print. The traces and consequences of such colonisation remain pervasive but the empire itself is in decline. It has been progressively incorporated into a far-reaching global transformation with a distinctively local meaning—the emergence of the dominion of signs.

The term 'dominion of signs' resists being assigned a single stable meaning and it is precisely this indeterminacy which I wish to exploit. Consider again the books, the rabbit hutch, the car(s) with which this text began. Add to them our daughters' rather different objects of veneration; the music, the clothes, the magazines, the television and radio programmes and the organised sport. However different these items are one from another what they have in common is that they are all signs. As such they are all ingredients in what Roland Barthes (1988, pp.157-9) has called 'the kitchen of meaning'. The world is full of such signs, but they are rarely simple and never innocent. Yet we are all routinely implicated in reading the messages they carry and in tacitly deciphering the social, moral and cultural values that they imply. One of the aims of this book is to slow down that acquisition of meaning and to subject it to scrutiny. The topics considered range from commercials to canonical literary texts but there is a particular emphasis on television. On one meaning then, 'dominion of signs' refers to this much enlarged notion both of what it is *to* read, and of *what* we read. This is less exclusive than the traditional emphasis on print, but it is none the less inclusive of print.

The associations of this first meaning are expansive; the implication is of an implicit but unacknowledged richness and complexity in popular texts and their interpretation. A second meaning shifts the emphasis away from readers as active constructors of culture and towards signs as a system of constraints. Far from being expansive, the term has associations of restriction and control, of narrow and narrowing disciplinary regimes which allow for a strictly limited amount of interpretative play in order to better secure consent to their regimen. Such structural constraints are seen as finding expression through the actions and interests of those responsible for the ownership, control and production of particular sign systems, or from properties intrinsic to their medium of transmission, or from the discourses which develop from the interaction of these factors. On this second meaning readers are primarily understood not as the interpreters of texts, but as constituted by them. Who the readers can be, and what they want are given by this larger system.[2]

In deploying these two meanings, the term 'dominion of signs' has been used to invoke the industries which organise the production of contemporary culture, *or* the audiences which recognise it, *or* the texts which realise it, *or* any combination of these. In the studies which make up this book there is a deliberate attempt to keep the tensions between these different starting points and interpretative emphases continually in play. This is one way in which the resources of cultural tradition, the claims of contemporary populism and the border patrols of different academic disciplines can be made to confront forms of complexity other than their own. A commitment to this kind of structured indeterminacy requires a text that intermittently calls attention to its own fictionality. This is, in Roland Barthes's phrase a 'healthy sign'. But rather than claiming this as the third meaning of 'dominion of signs', that phrase might better be reserved for the substantive topic which the studies themselves foreground, namely, the representation of New Zealand as a nation.

New Zealand as a country occupies a particular geographical location and in this sense it is a 'real place', its spatial boundaries defined and limited by state power. What could be more obvious, therefore, than the idea that there is a real New Zealand nation, consisting of real New Zealanders, whose essential defining attributes and characteristics can be mapped, just as the country's coastline can be mapped? A modern nation is, however, best understood through investigating what Anderson (1983, p.15) has called the style by which it is imagined. Such an 'imagined community' is grounded in material fictions which are produced and reproduced through various organised cultural instruments, institutions and practices. Anderson's particular focus is on the role played by novels and newspapers in constructing an imagined unity, identity and continuity over time amongst those they address. This is summarily sketched in his account of how the mundane daily ritual of reading the paper plays a crucial role in reproducing the social order:

> It is performed in silent privacy, in the lair of the skull. Yet each communicant is well aware that the ceremony he performs is being replicated simultaneously by thousands (or millions) of others of whose existence he is confident, yet of whose identity he has not the slightest notion. Furthermore, this ceremony is incessantly repeated at daily or half-daily intervals . . . At the same time, the newspaper reader, observing exact replicas of his own paper being consumed by his subway, barbershop or residential neighbours, is continually reassured that the imagined world is visibly rooted in everyday life . . . fiction seeps quietly and continuously into

> reality, creating that remarkable confidence of community in anonymity which
> is the hallmark of modern nations. (Anderson 1983, pp.39-40)

Man (as newspaper reader) is not a generic term. If the process which
Anderson evokes is recognisably gendered, then so too are the modes of
subjectivity which it fabricates and seeks to sustain. In New Zealand as
elsewhere constructing national identity has been largely a man's business, both a voice and an echo of the split between public and private.
In substantive terms the printing of nationalist legends has tended to be
refracted through images of war, work, sport, and politics which effectively positioned the reader as male. As such, the suppressed subtext of
the nationalist celebration of identity has always been the awareness of
difference.

This was further overlaid by that template which Andreas Huyssen
has called 'the Great Divide', and which lay between high (modernist)
culture and mass culture. It is something of a commonplace to note that
mass culture has been defined by the contrast with high culture. Initially,
the not-so-hidden subject matter of the mass culture critique was fear of
'the masses' themselves, a fear subsequently transposed by the argument
that the threat came not from below but from those who ran the relevant
industries. Huyssen's (1986) innovation is the suggestion that as mass
culture (and anxieties about it) developed towards the end of the nine-
teenth century, it was *also* inscribed with the properties of 'woman'. Within
the expanding domain of print culture, high culture's disciplined seriousness, its difficulty, its purported autonomy were said to distinguish it from
the passivity, dreaminess, frivolity and seductiveness, in short, the 'feminine' threat of mass culture. This cluster of connotations survived more
or less intact when 'the problem of mass culture' migrated from the Right
to the Left; when it changed from being seen as something driven from
below to being seen as something controlled from above. We have seen
that with the subsequent proliferation of the range and types of mass
media, the high/mass distinction itself has, in the eyes of Eco, Huyssen
and others, long since unravelled. Yet the legacy of this persistent gendering
of what was both devalued and feared nonetheless extends into the present.
Real critics don't read romances or watch soaps, which means that the
ambiguous pleasures of these entertainments are recognised 'only' by
millions of fans and a handful of academics (e.g. Modleski 1982; Radway
1984; Brown 1990).

One of the themes of this book is to identify how key elements of this high/mass culture distinction were replicated *within* the cultural project of New Zealand nationalism as it was carried forward by New Zealand writers and intellectuals in the immediate pre- and post-war period. In its claim to have identified the 'real New Zealand', the high-culture version of cultural nationalism effected a further displacement within the mass culture critique. It introduced a sub-textual fear of 'the foreign', as this was expressed in popular preferences for the derived and second-hand pleasures of imported culture. It thereby reiterated similar concerns expressed by some English cultural commentators about Americanisation, deploying them within a narrative in which fear of 'the masses' (subsequently suitably transmuted into 'the bosses') and fear of 'the feminine' were already at work (cf. Carter 1990). The permutations, tensions and dislocations thus set up within this emergent discursive field were contained and controlled by an emphasis on the discovery, creation and celebration of the indigenous and the individual. In terms of both form and content this (eventually) rendered it highly vulnerable to Maori and feminist critiques.

The high-culture identification of 'the real New Zealand' was always a fiction. That it could not have been otherwise is the fourth meaning of the 'dominion of signs'. That dominion presumes a mode of understanding which does not ask to what extent a particular conception of New Zealand is or was true, but rather focuses on the question of just how that conception is or was made to work. As such it is concerned less with explaining the New Zealand facts of life than with tracing the life of fictions in this place; looking for signs of life in the life of signs. Thus the fiction of 'the New Zealand tradition' was not *reducible* to the elaboration of hierarchical distinctions within the reign of print, or to a general privileging of print in relation to other media. It was, however, sustained by and dependent upon such processes. That narrative has subsequently been hollowed out from within and undercut from without.

Read one way, this book is about the fissuring and fragmenting of that tradition and the associated changes in the styles of national imagining. Read another, it is about how such changes are inexplicable without a recognition of changes in the technical means available for their delivery and the circumstances of their reception. Read yet another, it emphasises the plurality of selected popular texts, of how they are at once expressions of an irreducible indeterminacy and complexly coded manifestations of social change. More generally, it is about how to read now and about how we (sometimes) do read; about how to both use and interrogate the inherited and the imported; about how to play the gap between cosmo-politan and local in ways that take pleasure in probing for the parochi-alism of the former and unearthing the global complexity of the latter.

This is, to be sure, a nationalism of sorts, but it is one which, in principle at least, is agnostic towards questions of origin yet, in practice, tends to be in collusion with the pattern of local readings. It is something less than a reply to Eco's puzzle as to just 'what is going on?' As Eco recognises, for the answers to that query we have to begin by asking each other. But one implication of the dominion of signs is that our cultural preferences characteristically act as messages to others, that they function as a kind of language. Viewed in this light, the texts which are the subjects of this study are a proxy for talk, a conversation by other means amongst those who will never meet. But like the bizarre juxtapositions and collage of valued choices and products that are characteristic of the Perry household, they are brought together and held in place through conventions and tacit understandings that are mysterious to outsiders, unexplicated by their adherents and resistant to translation. In this book there is an attempt to uncover some of the relevant codes which are operative at the national level.

This argument begins with the account in Chapter Two of how tel-evision has transformed the production of cultural identity, focusing on such initiatives as Telethon, the handling of the '81 Tour, the KZ7 campaign and the comedy of Billy T James. The emphasis is on the attempts to both acknowledge and reconcile the wider social divisions of class, gender and ethnicity by their mode of representation within the television texts themselves. Chapter Three extends this approach to an analysis of the contrast between rural and urban in New Zealand and its representation in *Mortimer's Patch*, *Shark in the Park* and Barry Crump's commercials for Toyota pickup trucks. In Chapter Four it is further amplified through an exploration of images of Australia in New Zealand television commercials. Chapter Five revisits the theme of Chapter Two by foregrounding a Steinlager All Black commercial which is particularly knowing in its revamping of a traditional subject. The text which results is seen as a model example of modes of representation. Chapter Six takes the BBC's *The Singing Detective* as its subject matter in order to confirm the cognitive and other possibilities opened up by a provincial location and the associated modes of reading developed in earlier chapters. Chapter Seven brings these lessons to bear on the development of New Zealand fiction, somewhat in the spirit of Mark Poster's (1990, p.65) memorable but Delphic aphorism that 'deconstruction may better be defined as TV viewing applied to books'. The eighth and concluding chapter sketches the fate of literary versions of cultural nationalism in the 1980s by focusing on the decline of the *Listener*, the rise of *Metro* and the fantasy life of local management writers.

Most of the substantive material has previously appeared in essays which were written for specific occasions and audiences and which therefore operated in different registers. In preparation for this book they have all been through-written, i.e. amended or extended, revised and cannibalised so as to form part of a cumulative and more general argument. The original versions were typically responses to the textual expression of cultural changes as those changes were occurring. In reworking them for present purposes, I have sought to rescue something of what, at the time of writing, was the sense of a still open and indeterminate present, from what is now its relegation and subordination to the established pattern of the past. And rather than acquiescing to that flattening out of the prose which is the stigma of 'sounder' modes of academic practice, I have sought to retain something of those speculative, fluid and combative features which the essay form uniquely permits. What I have also sought to retain are those differences in tone which derive from variation in subject matter. As Chapters Five and Seven are designed to demonstrate, there are productive critical possibilities in reading such formally innovative texts as Frank Sargeson's early short stories and the 1987 Steinlager All Blacks television commercial together. But to *write* about them in the same way would be not merely wayward, but a foolish neglect of everything about their production, distribution and reception which makes them different. Each chapter may therefore still be read as a self-contained essay, albeit written at different levels of difficulty.

An overarching theme of contemporary literary theory is that authors are particularly untrustworthy and unreliable guides as to how their work should be read. And an overriding theme of studies of contemporary popular culture is that texts are frequently read in ways that their authors do not anticipate. In either event, the book does *not* stop here. Instead, what follows is a critical, enthusiastic complicity with some signs of the times.

1   Bloom's book was at one point number two on the US hardcover bestseller list during 1987.

2   From such a perspective to read critically is therefore seen as deriving either from the (roughly speaking, structuralist) attempt to construct and inhabit an imaginary space outside that system; or from the (roughly speaking, post-structuralist) attempt to (dis)locate the inconsistencies that are immanent in all such systems, using tactics which are highly reflexive as to their own contingent status.

TWO

Cinderella and the Silver Mercedes

Popular Culture and the Construction of National Identity

Within the dominion of signs the medium of exchange is fiction. It is, however, myth which provides the material backing, especially the myth of untold wealth and happiness. All the best fairy tales are based on the gold standard. In what is perhaps the most famous of all such stories, the heroine's chance to escape from deprivation and subordination depends upon the magical transformation of a golden pumpkin into a golden coach. The New Zealand variant that I want to tell begins with a silver fern and ends with a silver Mercedes. In this local version the metamorphosis of rugby's emblem into the icon of KZ7's Auckland homecoming, the transition from All Black magic to Kiwi Magic, depended upon the wider magic of television. And instead of a fairy godmother skilled in the practice of alchemy, there was a corporate godfather who succeeded in transmuting public relations into patriotism. In each of these Cinderella stories the magical effects were, of course, temporary—and therefore the associated assurance that 'she'll be right' seemed to be more an expression of hope than a sign of experience. What is clear, however, is that such effects can be read as signals of more enduring changes in the circumstances of our heroines and of those who eagerly identified with them. Thus, in his well-known study of fairy tales, Bruno Bettelheim (1976) argued that such fables deal with the emotional turmoil of growing up, with feelings of smallness and helplessness, with anxieties about the precariousness of identity, about strangers, about the external world and about the future.

Although I share Bettelheim's interest in what he calls 'the uses of enchantment', both the methodology and the focus of this chapter are rather different. My concern is a sociological one: to explore just how it is that shifts in dominant social imagery might indirectly map, and in turn be mapped onto, the continuities and changes in our collective life. I hope to demonstrate that during the 1980s the uncertain public profile of rugby, the rise and decline of Telethon, the marketing of KZ7 and the success of Billy T James were closely interconnected phenomena.

Rugby provides a starting point because the amount of cultural freight that it carried for so long depended upon the significance of the socio-logical task that it once performed. Thus, what emerges from Geoff Fougere's (1981) elegant analysis of the game is that rugby's one-time efficacy as a symbol of the New Zealand nation derived from its practical effectiveness as a mechanism of social integration.[1] He described how the game induced participation (and the identification that comes with it) through a relatively egalitarian team structure that linked men together despite those differences in their social background (such as social class and ethnicity) which might otherwise divide them. The competitive relation between local clubs provided the basis for their unification at the provincial level, and in their turn the competing provincial teams pro-vided the players for the national side. It is a model example of a familiar sociological process. The loyalties and sentiments of otherwise disparate and dispersed social actors were forged into an expression of national unity embodied in the All Blacks.

This whole process was not only built painstakingly from the bottom up, it was also coextensive with the emergence of New Zealand as a nation. As Fougere (1981, p.12) puts it, 'Before we had anything resem-bling a national market, or even a very effective national state, rugby tied together the collection of localities and provinces into a national body.'

That women appeared to be excluded from this mutual interpenetra-tion of mateship, nation-building and rugby was perhaps one of the rea-sons why the resulting conception of national unity came to seem well-nigh immaculate to its adherents. Women might be expected to work for rugby, but only men were expected to play it. Women's relation to the game was thus defined by and through the pattern of their relation to men, and rugby's ability to bridge the divisions between men was linked to men's capacity to prescribe subordinate roles for women.

For rugby and national identity to remain synonyms presupposed that the social and cultural distinctions between men were not too great and that the relations between men and women continued to be organised along traditional lines. The slow hollowing out of both of these premisses was a development which gathered momentum during the 1970s. Ethnic, class, gender and regional differences began to cut across that presumption of cultural homogeneity which rugby had helped to construct and to enforce. With these developments came a decisive broadening in the social base of the long-standing critique of rugby's South African connection. Moreover, realignments in this country's web of international dependencies meant that support for All Black rugby by organised economic and political interests, even when it was given, could no longer be taken as simply given. Finally, initiatives internal to the game highlighted the increasing pressure for it to operate less like a voluntary association and more like a commercial enterprise. Its founding principles of diffuse social involvement and amateur administration were being decisively undermined by a more obviously calculating interest in maximising spectators, employing players and professionalising management (de Jong 1986).

The lack of fit between emerging social patterns and those which had long been characteristic of rugby were therefore evident on a number of levels. The resulting pressures were at once internal and external, affecting both the game and the nation it purported to represent. By 1981 the empirical traces of these social forces were visibly coalescing and colliding on our streets and on our screens. The intensity with which rugby was defended not only signalled the sport's distance from the mantle of cultural representation but its closeness to the support of political repression. The game was no longer a central mechanism of social integration; it had become instead a measure of our social division.

If television revealed less of this than Merata Mita's 1983 film *Patu* or Ross Meurant's (1982) book, it did not and could not choose to conceal it. For television is arguably the most culturally central institution precisely because it is impelled by its very conditions of production to locate, or rather to construct and to seek to hold some notion of a middle ground. Television is too intent on maximising audiences to ignore popular sentiment, too important to the powerful for them to ignore it, and too interested in developing a measure of institutional autonomy to unambiguously subordinate itself to the expectations of either of these constituencies. The working solution to these contrasting pressures is a professional ideology of 'balance'. That this notion and the associated middle-ground metaphor are deeply problematic is evident from a number of studies of the medium (eg. Hall 1976; Kumar 1975; Wood 1984).

Television's middle ground is not some kind of virgin territory presided over by a neutral arbiter, but rather a site of struggle in a larger war of position in which the weapons are words and images. The ideas of 'balance' and 'middle ground' are no less ideologically charged than such notions as Muldoon's ordinary bloke, Nixon's silent majority, Rousseau's general will, and Plato's noble lie. But because the 1981 Springbok Tour divided us so deeply and so evenly, television could not but express that fact. The medium was driven to reaffirm its own culturally central location by presiding over the decentering of rugby.

The argument so far is that rugby's culturally privileged position had rested upon social foundations which were subject to an accelerating rate of erosion during the 1970s. At the same time, television was engaged in orchestrating and responding to that distinctive pattern of social practices which is New Zealand's Telethon. What was developed during this period was a local form of access television which powerfully articulated the medium's implicit claim to the position of cultural custodian. Rugby's centrality had derived from the way it had once acted as a major means of accomplishing social integration. That is to say, it was a social process for reconciling the maintenance of social order with the diverse characteristics and divergent interests of individuals and groups. The institution of Telethon simulated this sociological feat. But through its mode of simulating social integration, Telethon could also be said to have accomplished it. It accomplished it in the only sense possible in a society characterised by a much more developed division of labour, increased cultural complexity and emerging patterns of social division. It is that achievement—and its limits—which I want now to examine.

Telethons are no more unique to New Zealand than the cockfights which Geertz (1974) so eloquently describes are unique to Bali. But what is unique, and uniquely important is their respective cultural meanings and significance. Viewing figures for the local telethons screened from 1975 onwards throughout the 1980s have at times exceeded 70 per cent of the population, and the level of per capita donations for the 1978 Telethon got it into the *Guinness Book of Records* (three million dollars from three million people). How was such a phenomenon *possible*? What were the cultural conditions under which it could not only take place but *make sense*?

The main architect of Telethon, Don Hutchings, hints at where such an inquiry might begin. He once described Telethon as 'access television at its best'. The very phrase 'access television' enshrines a dilemma, for the notion of access and the institution of television embody rival tendencies of action. 'Access' implies broad-based communal involvement and meaningful local participation; 'television' implies a system of organisational control and a strategy of professional dominance. Given that the former is democratic in intent, whereas the latter is centralist by design, Telethon might therefore be seen as a distinctively local articulation of the Soviet ideal of democratic centralism. This whimsy does not, of course, mean that what Keith Sinclair once called 'the South Pacific's three million Prussians' somehow became the South Pacific's three million Russians. Rather what could be identified in Telethon was the visual and verbal representation of a society that is both committed to capitalism and disturbed by its consequences. Let me develop this.

The cultural legacy which rugby had helped to construct embodied a presumption of cultural homogeneity. Telethon moved and worked at the intersection between that presumption and a developing perception that it was threatened. My interest is therefore twofold. First, to explain how differences in motives, diversity in cultural practices, distinctions in social position and dispersed spatial locations were reconstructed and reconciled through Telethon. Second, to show how wider social changes have combined with the evolution of Telethon's own narrative principles to place limits on what it could accomplish and posed threats to its future. My argument is that Telethon engaged with pre-existing differences in sentiment, cultural practices and location, prised them loose from their origins, translated them into the homologous language of money and then redistributed them in a symbolic celebration of market values and a cultural construction of national unity.

In order to make that cryptic claim more explicit I want first to consider how the diversity of motives for popular participation in Telethon were transcribed and transformed through the development of a pattern of competitive giving. It was through this pattern that the real conditions of communal life and its simulation on Telethon were linked together, in ways that Geertz (1974) might recognise.[2] This depended upon Telethon's presenters routinely evaluating financial contributions by reference to the interaction of two criteria: the size of the donation and the perceived social status of the donor. The mark of a deep donation was that it exceeded the expected relation between monetary value and the donor's social position. That expected relation in its turn was structured through the competitive character of the giving. This was expressed both in the explicit 'challenges' issued by donors themselves to others of comparable status to match or better their contribution and in the interventions of media professionals engaged in orchestrating the standards applicable to a given social category of donors. The incentive to go deep was reinforced by the rising monetary tally on the national scoreboard. The possibility of altruism was thus forged into a simulation of the market, albeit aided and abetted through the intervention of agents of the state. However diverse the motives for giving might have been, they were routinely recruited as incentives for, and a reinforcement of, status competition. For individual, group and communal donors, the movement which Telethon enacted was always from gift to exchange.

In the case of contributions and representations from large corporations, however, this movement was arrested. The conventional pattern was that corporate donors expressly referred to their subordination to Telethon itself, and by implication to the social order which it represented. Corporate recourse to the rhetoric of community was part of a commercial grammar. The companies were invariably 'pleased to support . . .' or 'proud to take part in . . .'. An allocation from the advertising budget was presented as an expression of community values; and there were no 'challenges' from Fletcher Challenge or our other major companies. Moreover, the form of their contribution was as often in kind as it was in cash, such as the provision of facilities, materials, transportation or services.

The interventions of Telethon's media professionals served to further sublimate, if not suppress, the commercial content of such practices. This occurred by way of the proxy advertising which acknowledgements of support represented. Corporate giving was predetermined prior to transmission, so exhortation was inappropriate, but by comparison with individual or group donations it was substantial, so expressions of gratitude were in order. The big money helped to ensure that going deep was reinforced amongst those discretionary sources of donation which represented the target of Telethon's presenters. The big companies *did* compete on Telethon, not through the conspicuous display of their economic power, but through the struggle to gain access and get mentioned during prime time.

It is, however, in the realm of production and the world of paid employment that corporate interests and ordinary men and women face each other under conditions where their rival priorities are most likely to be evident. Many Telethon collections occurred at the workplace and typically derived their impetus from the actions of employees. The communalities which they expressed, and which had work groups as their focus, were visually displayed or verbally acknowledged (or both) in their Telethon appearances. What typically happened was that two or more employees were present for the purpose of presenting their total donation, or there was an explicit acknowledgement of indebtedness to co-workers. Whenever employees of small businesses and the individual branches of larger ones appeared on Telethon, their communal sentiments could and did spontaneously transcend the technical, hierarchical and social divisions characteristic of the world of work. The initial perception of such businesses was thus filtered through the metaphor of community. On Telethon the conflict of interest between capital and labour was either contained by this imagery or expressed, but typically controlled, by the symbolic invocation of a presumption of parity. This latter took the form of a donation from management which matched, dollar for dollar, that which had been collected by the workforce.

I have suggested that Telethon reconstructed the diverse motives of ordinary men, women and children into a celebration of the market, and the calculative motives of corporate donors into expressions of civic virtue. It also translated social activities into commercial values. Verbally this was accomplished through the question sequence characteristic of interviews with participants, which typically took the form 'who are you?' 'what did you do?' and 'how much did you get?' In making the connection between a given social activity and its fundraising consequences, the tag '-athon' became the conventional linguistic procedure. The function of '-athon', as in knit-athon, jog-athon, chess-athon, was to act as the bridging term between diverse and otherwise divergent social activities and the homologous language by which they were measured and weighted. It encapsulated the doctrine that money talks.

Whenever the social activities attendant upon fund-raising could be rendered compatible with the conventions of television entertainment, they might be displayed rather than merely described. The resulting transition from 'Telethon as documentary' to 'Telethon as entertainment' was signalled in a number of ways. The printing of pledge names and

Integrating the communal and the commercial: New Zealand's Telethon (1981).

acknowledgements on the bottom of the screen was suspended. The camera work indicated a more active editorial stance. The cutting was faster, cameras zoomed, panned and tracked, and lighting and set design were more in evidence. The ways in which ethnic minorities expressed their identity, or communal organisations their distinctiveness, were thus assimilated to television's entertainment code.

Integral to that code is the star system, indicated by the presence on Telethon of professional and (normally) highly paid entertainers. By employing distinctive visual conventions in the construction and presentation of items as entertainment, Telethon did not just recruit the non-commercial cultural practice, the unpaid amateur, and the professional entertainer to a common framework and basis for evaluation by viewers. It also posited a preferred ranking of these activities which was informed by commercial conceptions of value. Rank was signalled not by the duration of time before the cameras but by temporal location. That is to say, amateur and professional alike might get equal time, but 'prime time' was largely a professional preserve (albeit shared with the corporate and other major donors operating in Telethon's 'documentary' mode). Though the surface structures of amateur, folk or ethnic expression may have been little changed, the change in the context in which they appeared changed the meaning of such social practices. Their relocation within a different framework of conventions meant that they could no longer be seen as *sui generis*, or as outside of market relations. The effect was to redefine such performances as (more or less prestigious) commodities.

The most highly ranked professional entertainers were the overseas guests, especially those with their own show or series which had appeared on New Zealand screens. Within Telethon's entertainment code, they were an expression of our cultural dependence on metropolitan centres. But they also participated in the documentary code as panel members and audience interviewers. When they were face to face with New Zealanders in this way (whether they were viewers or Telethon participants), then the hierarchical rankings were subverted, for the promise of donations was often made dependent upon overseas guests behaving in ways that indicated that they did not consider themselves different. The display of social distance was not permitted. A (documentary code) principle of interpersonal egalitarianism was thereby made to coexist with a pattern of structured inequality (integral to the entertainment code)— and the instrument whereby such egalitarianism was accomplished was money. At the close of Telethon the rankings were not merely subverted but reversed: the overseas guests were then expected to tell us how wonderful we were.

Telethon's network structure of control allowed it to collapse distribution in space into the allocation of time. By the 1980s there was not one Telethon but six; each of the main metropolitan centres produced its own. National coverage was all but complete, but local and regional distinctiveness could be retained as most of what was transmitted in a given region was also produced there. A small percentage of each region's output was, however, networked and thus seen throughout the country. In their network appearances each centre strove to show itself as a model of communal enthusiasm. What the national Telethon thus signalled was local distinctiveness and regional rivalries. These were, however, bracketed and symbolically controlled by the new (and rising) total on the national scoreboard which usually marked the return to regional transmission. Within each region the contrast between urban and rural donations suggested that on a per capita basis the contributions from rural areas were disproportionately high. On Telethon this greater level of rural donations became a synonym for community itself and a benchmark for other locations and other groupings. That particular practice might be said to summarise the underlying theme of this section of my argument. Telethon gathered together the multiple meanings of community—that much abused, much overworked term that nonetheless still conveys the primordial image of social life—and made money their measure.

Telethon was not an imitation of our social life but a way of rendering it intelligible. My necessarily simplified reading of it suggests that its distinctive properties derived from the struggle to reconcile popular sentiment, corporate interests and broadcasting ideology. This is why it can be said to have simultaneously fulfilled and betrayed New Zealand's dream of itself, for the contradictory strands which were woven into Telethon cut across the predicates of that dream, that is, the assumption of common aspirations and shared social condition. While Telethon's content sometimes communicated a promise of transcendence and of cultural equality, its narrative organisation signalled structural inequality and centralised control. In Telethon's heyday, each of these contradictory impulses carried its own kind of social necessity. They were expressive of the balance of social forces at work in both access television and society.

They meant that all of Telethon's participants, including those media professionals otherwise predisposed to critically distance themselves from the action, were constrained to act as if they had internalised the principle of cultural equality. Yet even the most enthusiastic of Telethon's participants were constrained, not just by the general conditions of television production, but by narrative principles specific to Telethon, and which were themselves consistent with structural inequality.

There are parallels between such an interpretation of Telethon and what some cultural critics have identified as the defining characteristics of New Zealand literature. Thus some forty years ago Chapman (1973, p.75) suggested that in this country 'each author is driven to be his own sociologist'. He argued that the most general technique of presentation chosen was that of 'the participating "I" (a narrator), who tells his experience . . . from an angle of vision the constriction of which is informative but negatively so. For a New Zealand writer to choose the technique of omniscient narration would disperse the emotional force engendered by participation and constriction while letting the writer in for the whole task of drawing the social diagram' (Chapman 1973, p.77). In discussing Frank Sargeson's application of this technique, Copland (1973, p.53) argues that 'his most distinctive power as a writer is to contrive situations whose symbolic implication is rich for the reader but more dimly, if at all, discerned by the actors . . . The problem is how to reconcile the authorial range and the character range.'

The methodological lesson proposed here is that a reading of a collectively produced text such as Telethon should be no less sympathetic than that which these critics offer with respect to their preferred authors. This would allow for a recognition that Telethon routinely succeeded in addressing and appealing to real feelings and was routinely able to mobilise authentic human sympathies, while routinely doing damage to personal dignity. Its internal dynamic, and its accomplishment, was the product of a tension between the communal and the commercial and of the associated struggle to achieve cultural convergence. That achievement, and its future, were threatened by tendencies which derived directly from its popular success. Let me try and isolate two such threats.

First of all, we have seen how Telethon represented an attempt to locate and construct a notion of cultural centrality under conditions of increasing social differentiation and division. Through its purported goal of collecting for the sick, the disadvantaged or otherwise dependent, it served to tell us how lucky we were and how healthy was the state of our social life. But both the increased visibility of social divisions and Telethon's success have edged it towards the lines of cultural cleavage. The dilemma became one of how to identify an objective that is socially consequential and yet safe from social controversy. This was exemplified by the goals of the Family Trust, which provided the rationale for the 1983 Telethon. The 'Family at Risk' was close to home, but home truths were, and *had to be* fudged. Whatever might be a source of contention—women's rights, abortion, sex education and contraception for teenagers, euthanasia— could not be included as an aim. No risks were taken in defining the family at risk. Anything other than a consensual, and therefore limited, definition would have threatened to both rupture the narrative and limit the flow of donations.

The second problem derived from the progressive encroachment of business interests concerned to use Telethon for their own particular purposes. The effect was to subvert that very tension on which Telethon depended. The prospect, which gathered momentum through the 1980s, was that by a process analogous to Gresham's Law, the big money could drive out the little, thus threatening the community involvement that goes with the latter.

These seem to me the main reasons why Telethon could be said to have peaked, both culturally and in real monetary terms, in 1981.[3] When combined with BCNZ's financial preoccupations (and hence their reluctance to incur the costs of a project like Telethon), especially in the post-1989 broadcasting environment, they explain why we may not get another.[4]

Moreover, by the mid-1980s some of our larger corporations had discovered a different tack—one that was designed to take us all to Fremantle. It was nonetheless clear that the first of the Bank of New Zealand's television commercials in support of the America's Cup challenge sought to maintain continuity with, and thereby capitalise upon, Telethon's cultural accomplishments. The significance of this commercial for present purposes lies not in its similarities with Telethon but in its differences, for what merits attention are the means by which Telethon's themes were appropriated and deployed for novel purposes. The local success of Bob Geldof's 1985 global telethon had made it clear that there were powerful incentives to engage in the cultural equivalent of going offshore. Live Aid relocated the telethon idea in the context of an international competition for funds. It showed how it was possible to breath some new life into a famine-threatened Africa *and* New Zealand's own socially threatened 'one people, one nation' premiss.

In like fashion, the first BNZ commercial for the America's Cup implied that, by 'sailing away', the economic interests of some of New Zealand's fledgling multinational companies and the cultural anxieties of middle New Zealand might be brought together. It pushed the theme that successful participation in international competition depended upon national unity and could be used to secure it. But the process necessarily eschewed those pre-existing types of participation associated with rugby and Telethon by which such unity had been built. The dilemma it addressed was that of how to construct a Telethon for the rich, how to reconcile a socially consequential project with the private appropriation of its benefits. It required consumers certainly, spectators perhaps, donations if possible, but participants not at all. Involvement in the project was the subject of private arrangements and insider trading (cf. Gooding 1987). The requirement was that indicators of Telethon's particularities be preserved but that its central contradiction, the tension that was the source of its vitality, must be stilled.

My emphasis is on how that process is attempted right from the opening shot. The camera speeds rapidly across the shining sea; on the soundtrack a woman's voice sings the opening bars of 'Pokarekareana'.[5] As the camera closes on a spit of land, a solitary figure stands at the juncture of land, sea and sky. The short dissolves into a view of her softly lit face as she sings. She is Maori, and the implication is that she is wearing traditional dress. The next shot is of popular singer Dave Dobbyn singing to the camera. In the background is the entrance to a wharenui. On the soundtrack the tune remains the same but not the words: we are now listening to 'Sailing Away',[6] a song whose lyrics emphasise the 'one people' theme and the vessel as its expression. Dobbyn is joined by Billy T James and then by Tim Finn, but their arrival is intercut with both a detailed and a general view of a twelve-metre racing yacht under sail. Subsequent shots show a series of entertainers, media personnel and sporting personalities, both men and women, both Maori and Pakeha, intercut with yet more views of the boat (KZ5). It is not necessary that we recognise all the people on screen, only that we recognise the principles of representation—gender, ethnicity, sport, entertainment. Children are shown towards the close of the commercial—the camera first singles out a brown-eyed, dark-haired Maori boy and subsequently a blue-eyed, blonde-haired Pakeha girl. (Compare this with how the commercial's opening shots of a dark-haired, brown-eyed Maori woman singer cuts to a blonde, blue-eyed Pakeha male singer.) As the commercial develops, so the intercut shots of KZ5 progressively pull back from detailed to more general views of the vessel, with the camera's aerial location allowing it to swing lyrically through some of the later shots.

This orchestration of social symmetry, abetted by the appropriation of Maori motifs, is, I think, transparent enough. So too, is the attempt to establish a connection between the nation thus signified and the local challenger for the America's Cup. An interpretation which is content to stop at this point is, however, far from satisfactory. The feelings which such commercials are designed to mobilise are 'the very coinage of our brains'.[7] Those feelings cannot be quarrelled with, and ought not to be misanthropically mocked. The difficulty is how to isolate and understand the insidious practices whereby such sentiments are invoked, and so liberate them from the uses that the commercial makes of them. This requires a shift of attention away from its content and towards its form.

Consider, for example, the conventions governing *movement*. The people in the ad are shown as either standing still or moving only very slowly and then towards the camera. But the opening shot was from a camera that was racing across the water—an opening that is all but identical, incidentally, with the introductory frames of *Miami Vice*. The people may be immobile, but the boat is always shown as on the move, and in the later shots that sense of movement is enhanced by swinging the camera itself. The attempt to signify the integration of vessel and society thus depends upon the boat being shown through predominantly active principles of representation, and the social being shown through predominantly passive ones. Uniformities of rhythm and pace in the cutting serve to enhance this integrative effect. What is encoded is the suggestion that (to paraphrase Carlyle) we all 'lie still and think of New Zealand'. Moreover the ad moves to represent not only the stillness of those it portrays but their thinking too, this time through its alternation of full-face and three-quarter-face shots. Telethon's distinction between 'documentary' and 'entertainment' codes is here collapsed into a distinction between the ideal and the real within the single code of predominantly passive representations of the social. The ideal is signalled by three-quarter-face shots, the real by full-face ones. The chain of such

A telethon for the rich? BNZ's 1986 America's Cup campaign commercial. →

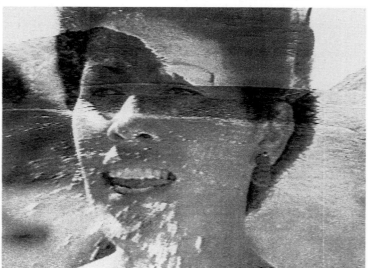

representations begins with the (traditional) ideal, moves to the real, briefly consolidates it, and then moves back to the (new) ideal. The three-quarter-face shot is deployed most frequently, for reasons which have been described by Roland Barthes in a waspish analysis of the portraits in electoral prospectuses. In his words:

> A three-quarter face photograph . . . suggests the tyranny of an ideal: the gaze is lost nobly in the future, it does not confront, it soars and fertilizes some other domain, which is chastely left undefined. Almost all three-quarter face photos are ascensional, the face is lifted towards a supernatural light which draws it up and elevates it to the realm of a higher humanity . . . the Olympus of elevated feelings, where all political contradictions are solved: peace and war, social progress and employers' profits . . . the Right and Left: all these coexist peacefully in this thoughtful gaze, nobly fixed on the hidden interests of Order. (Barthes 1973, pp.92-93)

That initial transition from ideal to real also marks the soundtrack's transition from traditional lyrics to new ones, from female to male, from Maori to Pakeha, and (within the limits of a predominantly passive code) from immobility to movement. Some restricted play is briefly permitted (you can see the attempts to break out, particularly amongst the professional entertainers, who have, of course, learned to invest their performances with some gusto), before being stilled by subsequent and more protracted recapitulations of the ideal. Since the subjects of representation are unchanged, what is encoded is the merging of real and ideal.

There is space to do no more than note that in the second commercial, 'The Challenge', which emphasises the vessel and its crew, and which has 'We're gonna pick it up' as its theme tune, there is much more action. The two commercials are linked through representations of the vessel and the appropriation of a Maori theme. But this commercial is a masculine preserve—there is therefore a positive sanctioning of aggression, and the cutting is much more rapid. As well as displacing domestic divisions into external competition, the commercial reconstructs traditional notions of masculinity on new terrain. It might thus be said to represent part of an attempt to replicate the functions once performed by rugby, but through a sport of which the practice is permeated by new high-tech indicators of masculine power, is more explicitly subordinate to commercial considerations, and where international sporting competition and economic interests work in tandem rather than in opposition.

And when this is wedded to what all but the most churlish recognise as KZ7's remarkable performance, then most of us can be reached.

In fact, crowd estimates for the Auckland welcome-home parade were as high as 200,000. In that parade a fleet of expensive German automobiles was used to transport KZ7's crew members down Queen Street. Many of those who turned out to cheer were office-workers and, by contrast with rugby, a clear majority were women. It is not surprising that a $300-a-week typist might view the back seat of a silver Mercedes as more attractive than the front of the stand at Eden Park. This is at once a commentary on what she believes her choices are, an observation on emerging patterns of seduction and a measure of how successful capitalism and patriarchy are in cleaning up (the image of) their act.

The intensity of the response to the America's Cup saga can, however, be read another way, as a mark of how deeply felt was the need to participate and how deeply it had been suppressed. Both the challenge organisers and the event itself confounded such desires; the crew and organisation were off limits, and as a spectacle it was not just off-shore but wholly reliant upon television. However imperfectly, and in however controlled a fashion, Telethon—and rugby before it—had constituted a kind of dialogue between various social forces. The marketing of KZ7 depended not upon dialogue but upon forms of closure that are characteristic of corporate interests which can no longer be described as simply ascendant, but have become politically and economically dominant.

That does not mean, however, that they have achieved cultural victory, and I want to invoke a definition of culture which challenges the unitary and utilitarian premises of the KZ7 commercials, but which is applicable to some of the most popular material on our television screens. The definition comes from the opening pages of Lionel Trilling's *The Liberal Imagination*:

> A culture is not a flow, nor even a confluence; the form of its existence is struggle, or at least debate—it is nothing if not a dialectic. And in any culture there are likely to be certain artists who contain a large part of the dialectic within themselves, their meaning and their power lying in their contradictions; they contain within themselves, it may be said, the very essence of the culture.(Trilling 1950, p.9)

Trilling's main candidates for that role are the American writer Henry James and the English novelist Jane Austen. My own local nominees are the entertainers Billy T James and Lynn of Tawa. I've space for only the briefest consideration of Billy T, and Lynn will have to wait for another occasion.

A preliminary approach to, and appreciation of, the complexity and subtlety of Billy T's public persona can be derived from the way various directors have traded on it. For example, in the feature film *Came A Hot Friday*, director Ian Mune typically introduces the Tainuia Kid by showing us only a gloved hand, his boots, or glimpses of him in the distance. The immediate roars of recognition on the occasion when I saw the film indicated that the audience bring to the character as portrayed their conception of Billy T himself. The screen character is thus consciously presented so as to work off, and be enriched by, the local audience's knowledge of the actor and the plurality of his roles. At the same time the character himself (a Mexican-Maori gunfighter played for laughs) embodies all sorts of contradictory cultural messages. Thus at one level Hollywood's parody of Mexicans is employed in order to parody Hollywood itself. This implies that, initially at least, the character of the Tainuia Kid might be read as a victim of (American) cultural imperialism—the colonised subject of a colonising culture. Yet the Kid's narrative role is to form part of the (successful) attack on home grown villainy—a role in strict accordance with Hollywood conventions. This duality in narrative function is, moreover, further dislocated by a subtext which plays upon the structural similarity between the Hollywood/Mexican relation and the Pakeha/Maori one. The theme of coloniser and colonised is thereby invested with both a shared, externally focused meaning and an internal meaning which corresponds to a crucial local social division. A complex indeterminacy is thus conferred upon local readings of his narrative role and outlaw status. Rather than a passive victim of Americanisation, he is open to interpretation as an active indigenous subject, whose deployment of a parodied Hollywood image becomes a wry commentary on the dominant local culture and its modes of control.

The ambiguities of this role are echoed in Billy T's appearances in the children's television programme *Terry and the Gunrunners*, where he takes the part of an intellectual who happens to be a bikie (or a bikie who happens to be an intellectual). It is a performance which not only subverts assumptions about two of New Zealand's most deviant occupations by combining them together, but plays against Marlon Brando's role in *The Wild One* and mocks Rotary clubs by carrying an imitation of their insignia on his handlebars. If one compares the end result with his lacklustre equivalent in the book from which the programme derives, one begins to get a sense of the kind of cultural work which was achieved through (and by) Billy T. Thus his television commercial for the BBQ Factory was so layered and so resistant to a single reading that it would repay being looked at from the standpoint of Empson's classic *Seven Types of Ambiguity* (1930). It works like those Chinese box puzzles which Tom Stoppard builds into his plays. It presented two versions of Billy T: one wealthy, one not; one famous, one not. What we watch is a famous and wealthy entertainer playing a far from wealthy and anonymous character mocking a famous and wealthy character. ('He's got fat since he became famous, eh,' says the equally fat, but not famous central character for which Billy T James was, of course, famous.) The character who isn't wealthy *seems* to make a fool of himself, but he nonetheless gets the last word. Furthermore the contrast between the two characters personifies social change. But because it *personifies* it, it becomes not just a contrast between rich and poor but between a rich Maori and a poor one. Do we see the wealthy being mocked? or do we see a wealthy Maori being mocked? Do we see a reinforcement of negative stereotypes? or do we see them being subverted? Do we see a clumsy figure of fun, or a puncturer of pretensions? Do we laugh with, or laugh at?

The same sorts of questions were routinely raised by his television series. When he confides to the camera that he will 'show us how to get a cheap car from the Pakeha', and does so by making use of the car salesman's racism, or confronts Captain Cook's offer to trade trinkets with a Visa card sign, what is the basis of our response? Do we read these gems as evidence of incorporation or of opposition? as a testament to resourcefulness or as grounds for suspicion? The meaning spins away, and a single stable reading proves to be elusive. This ambiguity derives from the cultural resources with which the man worked, the diversity of his audience and the texture of his performance. He tacks back and forth between our social divisions and our points of contact, between mocking the Aussies and probing our own failings. By texture I mean the indications that behind each role there is always something else, something known but not said. It is, in part, a product of our awareness of the range and diversity of the roles that Billy T had previously played. But it also comes through as a kind of tacit challenge, as a suggestion that he should not be misconstrued. He is a man from one culture who has participated in, and succeeded by, the standards of another. I recognise that the

political correctness of such a practice is contested. My point is that for Billy T James himself the resulting ambiguities were *existentially* correct. And for the society which he entertained so well, those same ambiguities were as close to a cultural essence as our present divisions will permit.

The explicit focus of this chapter has been the ways in which changes in cultural imagery are at once fictional and linked to realignments in social relations. It has also sought to demonstrate that it is not just the content, but also the concept, of popular culture which is the subject of struggles between competing social forces. This is why popular culture should not be subsumed under the single undifferentiated category of mass culture, for the task of defining it is not just a matter of counting heads. It is precisely the signs of a struggle over content which distinguishes contemporary popular culture from the mass culture in which it is now embedded. Those same signs are also a means of recognising and reaffirming its much attenuated links with folk culture. 'Attenuated' because it is a characteristic of folk culture that those who produce it and those who consume it are (potentially) interchangeable and always members of the same group (cf. Kress 1976). In mass culture, by contrast, not only are producers and consumers discrete, but control over production is increasingly concentrated, whereas access to consumption is increasingly dispersed.

Contemporary popular culture is the place where these otherwise distinctive means of organising cultural practices meet. Its hallmark is that ordinary men and women are willing and able to make something of their lives with and through it, notwithstanding the fact that it is nowadays likely to be made for them, rather than by them. This seems remote from what the historian of popular culture, E. P. Thompson (1968), meant by his forceful advancement of the claim that the English working class 'made itself'. What could possibly reach across those differences (in time, in place, in organisation, and in social and political consequences) which separate the historical subjects of Thompson's study from their counterparts in contemporary New Zealand? What seems to me common to both is the notion of an active engagement under unpromising circumstances, a reminder to the powerful of what they are up against. Popular culture's relation to the dominant social order is characteristically a complex pattern of opposition, accommodation and evasion; it is an index of suppressed possibilities as well as a means of securing consent. On Telethon it can be glimpsed not only

← Essential reading for a divided culture: Billy T James's BBQ Factory commercial.

among the losers in this society but among the children. Between them they manage to make moral seriousness a source of pleasure and to show that dignity need not be dour. It is underlined by their bewilderment when one or more of Telethon's presenters behave as small children do when they know they are losing our attention. And it is confirmed by the glances of recognition occasionally evident among the handful of Telethon professionals who have not yet lost their way.

Thompson interpreted his task as that of recovering working people's lives from what he called the 'enormous condescension of posterity' (1968, p.13) My more modest aim has been to detect, and to try to subvert, some of the condescension of the present, whether it is manifest amongst those responsible for the production of mass culture or amongst those critics who view the popular with disdain. Against this, I have sought to show how popular culture 'reaches people where they live'. That expression has both the prosaic, matter-of-fact meaning of physical location, and the culturally profound one which Raymond Williams (1960) refers to as 'structures of feeling'. My quarrel is not just with those producers of mass culture who are at pains to blur the distinction between these two meanings, but with those high-culture critics who are unwilling to look for it, and with the pattern of complicity which is the result.

1 See also Fougere (1989). Crothers (1983) is a commentary and empirical extension of aspects of Fougere's initial argument.
2 The Balinese cockfight provides an improbable, but instructive parallel. In a fine essay Clifford Geertz describes how for the Balinese it is, or more exactly, deliberately is made to be, 'a simulation of the social matrix in which its devotees live' (Geertz 1974, p.18). The link is effected through the wagering which accompanies each cockfight. Centre bets are always even money bets, whereas side bets are asymmetrical, but the larger the centre bet the greater the propensity for side bets to be pulled towards the even money pattern. This is because the size of the centre bet is an index of the extent to which the cocks are evenly matched. 'Deep' matches are those with large centre bets and in such deep play 'money is less a measure of utility . . . than it is a symbol of moral import' (Geertz 1974, p.16). Money gambling is characteristic of shallow matches; in deep fights what is at stake is the status of the gamblers themselves. 'What makes Balinese cockfighting deep is thus not money in itself but what, the more of it that is involved, the more so money causes to happen: the migration of the Balinese status hierarchy into the body of the cockfight' (Geertz 1974, p.17).
3 The 1981 Telethon raised $5 million at the time of screening, a figure which was swelled to $6.2 million by late donations. At constant prices it therefore represented the largest of all those national telethons held since 1975.
4 TV3 produced its first telethon in 1993.

5 'Pokarekareana' has an unofficial status as New Zealand's national song.

6 During 1987 it became the biggest-selling record single in New Zealand's history.

7 The line is from *Hamlet*, Act 3, Scene 4, and refers to the ghost of Hamlet's father. It is precisely because such feelings are, in cognitive terms, simply non-negotiable, that they are, in advertising terms, so attractive a commodity.

THREE

Toyota Country and Toyota City

Urbanism and the Representation of Community

Raymond Williams's *The Country and the City* (1973) is a classic work by one of Britain's most accomplished cultural analysts. In its opening chapter ('Country and City') Williams begins by noting that in the English language 'country' can mean either the whole society or its rural area, and that 'city' is a synonym for civilisation. The substance of the book is an exploration of the contrasting feelings and associations which have gathered around these two terms, and an investigation of the changing relation between them, as this is expressed in works of English literature. The result is an interpretation of the historical development of a single society as represented in its fiction. What is portrayed is not just the general social transformation from an agrarian to an industrial society, but also the specific cultural meanings of that change as it is played out through changing attitudes to the country and the city.

In the book's closing chapter ('Cities and Countries') there is an explicit recognition that some of the main features of this historical sequence are effectively international, that the changes wrought in the countryside and the creation of cities are manifestations of a global process of reorganisation. But however general this process may be, it is everywhere mediated and modified by pre-existing patterns of local social organisation and necessarily accompanied by localised (if not always local) sentiments and beliefs. It is this incipient methodological stance which is of particular interest for the purposes of investigating the cultural imagery of urbanism and community in New Zealand. What it suggests is the appropriateness of a strategy which recognises the interplay between global structures, nation-specific institutional formations and culturally meaningful local narratives. This chapter is in accordance with such an approach. It begins by sketching out some selected structural characteristics of the urban pattern in this country, and then probing its portrayal within popular culture. Japan is used to highlight New Zealand's distinctiveness, since Japan is (roughly) similar in area to New Zealand but is dramatically different with respect to size of population and pattern of urbanism.

New Zealand's total population of less than three and a half million occupies a land area of 268,000 square kilometres. Hence whereas Japan has a population density of some 329 persons per square kilometre, the equivalent New Zealand figure is about 12. Nevertheless, like its Australian neighbour, New Zealand is one of the most urbanised nations in the world; in the 1986 census 83.8 per cent of the population was defined as 'urban'. But the extent of this urbanisation is in no way closely linked to the development of large-scale manufacturing or mass production. There are only a very few firms with more than a thousand employees and the typical industrial enterprise employs only a handful of people. Furthermore the entire country continues to remain crucially reliant upon agriculture, forestry and fishing for the great bulk of those export receipts upon which its economic wellbeing depends. A structurally distinctive feature of New Zealand's country/city relationship is therefore the combination of a strategically significant rural sector and a statistically dominant urban population.

This dependence upon the rural sector derives from the way in which the structure of the economy and the development of the nation were decisively shaped by its role as a British colony. The advent of refrigerated cargo consolidated New Zealand's place within the international division of labour. It became a producer of cheap food for a leading economic power on the other side of the globe. New Zealand was, and is, the world's most efficient producer of that relatively narrow range of primary products (notably wool and dairy produce) on which its prosperity has historically been based. By the 1950s, this had made it possible for its people to enjoy the third highest per capita income in the world. The engines of that prosperity were the many thousands of economically and spatially dispersed family farms, a system of production which could be, and was, made compatible with a relatively egalitarian income distribution.[1]

New Zealand is no longer in such a privileged economic position, having been overtaken by a score of countries. The very way in which New Zealand's comparative advantage was constructed meant that the country had been decisively linked into meeting the needs of just one overseas market rather than many. The combination of a narrow range of export commodities and a heavy dependence upon British consumers and the British connection was an indicator of continued colonial status and a recipe for economic vulnerability. From the 1930s onwards efforts were therefore made to broaden the basis of the economy through a strategy of import substitution. Domestic industries were sheltered from overseas competitors by way of an elaborate system of tariffs and quotas. A centralised and interventionist state, whose public works programme had earlier provided the infrastructure for agricultural development, expanded the range of its activities. This combination of import substitution and state expansion helped both to shape the pattern of urbanism and to accelerate its pace.

The physical appearance and organisational dynamics of New Zealand cities are rather different from those characteristic of either European or Japanese cities of comparable size or population. Factories and workshops (such as those which spread across South Auckland) grew under the umbrella of import substitution and are typically small in scale. Outside of the central business districts there are few buildings more than two or three storeys high. Suburban development (such as the commuter suburbs which house Wellington's bureaucrats) is more lateral than vertical. Urban locations show neither the sediments and traces of a preindustrial past, nor the kind of built environment that is characteristic of a Fordist industrial present or recent past. Thus although the Auckland conurbation is one of the largest cities in the world by area (comparable with Tokyo, Los Angeles and New York), its population is still just under one million people.

This apparently anomalous configuration of large area and low density dramatises a pattern of urbanisation that is echoed in New Zealand's other centres of population.[2] Throughout the nation the housing stock consists overwhelmingly of single, detached dwellings (each occupying approximately 800 square metres of land) occupied by their owners rather than rented. (At the time of the 1986 census 73.7 per cent of all dwellings were owner-occupied.) Historically the evolution of this pattern was dependent upon the state's provision of mortgage finance, but funding is now largely organised through private-sector loans. There are significant

vernacular elements in domestic house design, but the single most important architectural influence has probably been the California bungalow of
the 1930s. Both building styles and building materials have, however,
become more diverse in recent years, and there are discernible traces of
other sources and traditions including the Japanese.

Alongside New Zealand's low-density pattern of spatially dispersed
urban and suburban development is a high level of reliance upon the
private motor car as a means of transport. The OECD figures for 1971
show that there were 324 cars for every thousand people. This figure was
exceeded only by the USA with 443 vehicles, at a time when New
Zealand ranked fourteenth in the OECD in terms of per capita private
consumption (OECD 1975, appendix). By 1988 New Zealand per capita
consumption was $US6830 and the country had fallen to eighteenth
place, but there were now 490 cars per thousand people. This was still
lower than the US figure of 559, and just below Australia's, but more
than double that for Japan (241 per thousand), and much greater than
that for the United Kingdom (318 per thousand), although each of these
countries had per capita consumption well in excess of $US8000 (OECD
1990, appendix).

The extent of this dependence upon the automobile is also evident
from other data on travel patterns and household expenditure. The 1986
census indicated that 87.6 per cent of households used one or more cars
for private transport. Only 9.3 per cent of those travelling to full-time
work (6.7 per cent of males, 14.1 per cent of females) made use of public
transport, some 11.8 per cent used a company-supplied car (16.4 per cent
of males, 3.0 per cent of females) and 44.7 per cent used their own
vehicle (42.7 per cent males, 48.6 per cent females). The 1986–87 Household Expenditure Survey found that public transport accounted for just
1 per cent of such expenditure, whereas vehicle purchase, ownership
expenses and other private transport costs accounted for more than 13
per cent. Housing accounted for 21.6 per cent and household operation
and furnishing a further 13.8 per cent (NZ Dept of Statistics 1989, pp.171–
4).

New Zealand urbanism is thus a remarkably effective system for maximising a distinctive pattern of consumerism based on owner occupancy
and the private car. There is a low level of collective provision of services
such as transport and leisure facilities. Households also tend to contain
relatively few people, typically distributed across either one or two gen-

erations. These households are expected and exhorted to maintain extensive inventories of consumer durables and to undertake a wide range of maintenance activities. The general form of the built environment, the system of spatially dispersed, small scale households and the specific features of this consumerist culture pattern are mutually reinforcing.

Mullins (1981a; 1981b) documents a very similar urban pattern in his account of the Australian city. His guiding principle of theoretical selection was, however, just how such a pattern contributes to the reproduction of labour power. This chapter has a rather different emphasis. It foregrounds questions of cultural use and therefore has a more theoretically indeterminate focus on consumption. For example, the specifics of the local pricing system for private telephone rentals (a flat fee, with no limits on the number or duration of local calls) has probably had important consequences for the construction and maintenance of local networking.[3] Whether such networking reproduces or transforms the social structure is seen as an open question. In similar fashion, neither the cultural meaning nor the social effects of owner occupancy are here interpreted as theoretically given, not least because in New Zealand owner occupancy does not necessarily mean residential stability. As the number of suburban real estate offices implies, New Zealanders are nomadic, and the rationale for this process, and its relationship to the formation and reproduction of social classes and the processes of capital accumulation is a complex and empirically vexed one (cf. Smith & Thorns 1980). In a recent sixteen-nation study by the US Census Bureau, New Zealand had the highest rate of residential mobility (19 per cent per annum), an aggregate figure which masks the rapidity of turnover in some middle-class suburbs.

We have noted the widespread use of private means of transportation. The cars themselves are now overwhelmingly Japanese in origin. During the 1980s Japanese manufacturers accounted for between 60 and 80 per cent of all new car registrations (Lambert 1989, p.288). Toyota has emerged as the single largest seller. In the month of July 1991 it was responsible for some 24.9 per cent of new car sales. Its nearest rivals were Ford with 14.9 per cent, Mitsubishi with 14 per cent, and Nissan with 12 per cent. The cultural significance which attaches both to the house and to the car is, however, inflected through a local urban form which is very different from that of Japan. New Zealand may be Toyota country, but it is not Toyota City.[4] The contrast between the built environments of the two nations is also, in effect, a contrast between a situation in which car ownership is still discretionary (Japan)[5] and one in which it is all but obligatory (New Zealand).

Yet for many years there were severe restraints on the acquisition of both locally and overseas-assembled cars (a deposit in overseas funds, import licensing, high duties). Even as recently as the early 1980s the import duty on cbu (completely built-up) British vehicles was around 80 per cent and for others, including Japanese, it was a staggering 130 per cent. This policy was part of the import substitution strategy, designed to encourage a system of domestic assembly which made use of some locally made components. During the 1970s the number of local assembly plants increased from 10 to 16, following some relaxation of the restrictions on the importing of ckd (completely knocked-down) vehicle packs. Yet throughout the 1970s and 1980s the nation's new car sales averaged around 80,000 vehicles a year, and have only once (in 1973) exceeded 100,000 (Lambert 1989, p.277). Import controls have now been removed and tariffs drastically reduced. As a result, local new car prices are, for the first time, much closer to those characteristic of the main centres of vehicle production. Because of the most recent developments, New Zealand has also become the main overseas destination for second-hand cars originally built for, and used in, Japan itself (both countries drive on the left). In 1990, some 60,000 such vehicles entered the country.

The contradiction between the long-standing and internationally very high rate of vehicle ownership, (what was until recently) the highly inflated cost of a new car, and New Zealand's modest income levels proves to be more apparent than real. When supplemented by an awareness of the age distribution of the vehicles involved, it becomes rather less puzzling. Until well into the 1980s there was a very high proportion of older cars on New Zealand roads. In recognising that a car was both a practical necessity and a financial burden, the working solution of many ordinary New Zealanders was the resourceful maintenance and continued operation of a vehicle which elsewhere would have been sent for scrap. Hence the enthusiasm for used Japanese imports. Amongst the salaried middle class, the provision of a company car reached, and still reaches, much lower down in corporate hierarchies than anywhere else in the world.

Some of the empirical indicators of New Zealand's overall pattern of urbanisation have been sketched out, a pattern that is explicable as an articulation of global economic imperatives. This pattern is, in its turn, linked at the level of household organisation to a specific, if not wholly discrete, cultural system, a distinctive ensemble of capital goods, consumer durables and social meanings and practices. Read one way, its specificities can be seen as made possible by local choices; read another, it can be seen as made necessary by the particular position that New Zealand occupies within a global system.[6]

When viewed against Williams's distinction between the country and the city, the European settlement of New Zealand can be understood as a product of the extension of that distinction beyond the boundaries of the nation state. New Zealand as a country derived from the expansion of British cities; geographically it may have been in the Pacific, but structurally it was a part of Britain's rural hinterland. Coming with that settlement was an assorted collection of cultural baggage, so that New Zealand was not so much discovered as fabricated from pre-existing cultural categories. Whether New Zealand was constructed as material opportunity, as refuge, or as rural idyll, the space it occupied in the imagination of British settlers was already given by the culture from which they came.

It is the legacy of that process (cryptically formulated as 'profit, peace and perfection' by the novelist Maurice Shadbolt, 1980, p.191[7]), which was constituted and naturalised as 'New Zealand culture'. It had, of course, been complexly refracted through local contingencies, including the displacement and resistance of the indigenous Maori culture. In the early 1970s (when the moment of its cultural high-water mark had already passed), its popular expression was sardonically and affectionately captured in Austin Mitchell's satire, *The Half Gallon, Quarter Acre Pavlova Paradise* (1972). The title has associations with Tom Wolfe's classic celebration of American popular culture, *The Kandy-Kolored Tangerine-Flake Streamline Baby* (1965). Just as Wolfe had found a quintessentially American art form in customised cars, so Mitchell found the basis of a populist, egalitarian culture in the details of suburban living. Both before and since, high-culture critics have viewed what they saw as such suburban materialism with dismay, insisting on its meanness of spirit, its betrayal of possibilities, the narrowness of its content and the closure of its concepts—the selfsame charges that were subsequently brought against the selfsame high culture by feminist and Maori critiques.

These altogether grittier and more acerbic diagnoses now circulate alongside the sentimentality of a once semi-official populism. They posit a culture founded in, and upon, alienation and violence, and argue for the necessity of acknowledging and engaging with its implications and effects. If the specific intention of these various challenges may sometimes have been to substitute an alternate pattern of closure, the overall effect has been to open up a more plural, more contested conception of culture as a dynamic field of forces rather than an integrative unity.

Materially, however, the notion of a common culture has come under greatest pressure from the differential effects of economic reorganisation and structural change. The traditional slogans of that culture were that New Zealand is 'God's own country', and 'a great place to bring up kids'; that 'we are one people' committed to 'security and equality' and that 'she'll be right'. These and related sentiments were once part of a formally approved popular rhetoric of nationalism, understood and promulgated as cultural givens; any questioning of them was limited to arguing that they had, as yet, been imperfectly realised. What is now routinely questioned is not just their empirical status, but their appropriateness as social and cultural ideals.

The ongoing attempt to reconcile this threatened pattern of cultural beliefs with the prevailing form of urban organisation is undertaken via the idea and the ideal of 'community'. One of the reasons why the idea of community flourishes in the cultural imagination of New Zealanders is precisely because the material organisation of everyday life makes its routine enactment so problematic. This is another way of putting a point made in Chapter Two, where Telethon was seen as signalling a populace that was both committed to capitalism and disturbed by its consequences. Within such a society, the *idea* of community is a practical necessity, while its *realisation* would seem to be a practical impossibility. The combination of high rates of geographical mobility, the urban form and a privatised and instrumental pattern of social relations do not sit easily with those ties of kinship, interdependence and a settled allegiance to place which are the conventional markers of community life.

One of the ways in which the associated cultural dilemma is displayed is through a pattern of friendliness without friendship. This takes the form of a generalised, but nonetheless emotionally authentic, expression of sociability. It depends upon, and is thus limited by, the presumption of social similarity rather than a tolerance and exploration of the fact of personal difference. Amongst men it is, not unexpectedly, sustained by and inflected through local variants of those codes of emotional expression and control that are characteristic of hegenomic masculinity (cf. Gray 1983; Phillips 1987). But a study of women migrants (Baker 1979) suggests that the pattern may reach across the gender gap. Whilst confirming that New Zealand women did indeed seem friendly, the study's respondents also reported encountering tacit barriers and implicit controls which confounded efforts to establish relations of more depth.

In negotiating just where to draw the line between solitude and solicitude, or in trying to reconcile spatial mobility with emotional investment (itself a tellingly calculative metaphor), does this mean that the dominant local tendency is effectively to privilege the first terms over the second? Some cultural commentators have certainly thought so. One was even prompted to argue that New Zealanders were (and still are) a 'passionless people' (McLauchlan 1976); another had earlier suggested that they were akin to fretfully dreaming sleepers (Pearson 1962). But insofar as these analyses are constructed in terms of some general relation between culture and personality, they tend to both mislocate the problem and misinterpret its manifestations. In positing some kind of morally deficient national character (from which such authors and their assenting readers are miraculously exempt), they effectively transform what are, at best, somewhat contentious sociological generalisations into wholly spurious ontological claims. The effect is to direct attention away from both the institutionalised modes through which cultural expression characteristically occurs and the task of investigating their limits and limitations.

The sheer volume of cultural freight which the notion of 'community' is obliged to carry typifies it as one such mode. It is frequently invoked but rarely defined. At one moment it is the primordial image of social life, and at another that residual part of it which occupies the interstices between the formal economy and the bureaucratic state; both a utopian promise and a marginalised practice, both sociological bedrock and political vacuity. Whether as word or as referent, 'community' is therefore expected to do too much (unpaid) work.[8] But if the resulting rhetorical overload undermines the term's usefulness as an analytical resource, it enhances its interest as a topic. Precisely because of its very generality and indeterminacy, the notion of community acts as the repository for a raft of cultural anxieties and as a meeting point between multiple discourses. It is a cultural site at which New Zealand's manifest social and cultural differences confront not just one another, but the fact of difference and the legacy of (a presumed) cultural homogeneity. It is a blind spot by and through which a vision peculiar to the nation is expressed; a lie which tells the truth. This is a large claim. One way to briefly demonstrate it is by way of a (necessarily cursory) investigation of how community is constructed on locally made television.

The paradox of community identified here is integral to urban New Zealand. Yet on New Zealand television (as in New Zealand fiction and films) images of the rural have typically provided the source from which conceptions of community have been constructed. This echoes the British cultural pattern from which it derives (and which Raymond Williams's text explores). But we have seen that although most New Zealanders (like most of the British) live in towns and cities, the New Zealand countryside (unlike the British) is the main engine of the economy, and that there are systematic structural differences between the urban forms characteristic of the two nations. This means that New Zealanders both mobilise and read images of the rural differently from those societies whose wealth and wellbeing does not rest upon agriculture, and whose built environments display a more complete colonisation of the natural world. Under such conditions, the claim that 'rural New Zealand' somehow stands for national culture is therefore not wholly without plausibility. Notwithstanding the overwhelmingly urban audience, such a claim can better resist being defined as only marginal, or merely nostalgic, or unequivocally escapist, than is the corresponding notion of 'rural Britain'.

This is not, of course, to argue that the use of rural imagery in New Zealand-produced films and television is therefore natural or realistic. Even the vernacular celebration and documentary form of the popular *Country Calendar*, a television series now in its twenty-fifth year, depends upon a construction of the rural which is a collage of British antecedents, media-specific conventions, local inflections, particular social interests and material constraints (cf. Carter & Perry 1987). This is in no way intended to detract from *Country Calendar*'s achievement; on the contrary, it is a testimonial to it.

Country Calendar is distinguished by its longevity. It is, however, only one of the high proportion of television programmes, novels and films produced in New Zealand which have a rural subject matter. Given the small population, such local production forms only a small part of the total amount of material in circulation. What is striking is not the absolute number of such cultural products, but rather their relative importance. The nation's favourite cartoon strip (*Footrot Flats*) is set on a farm, and *Mortimer's Patch*, a popular television police series in the early 1980s, was centred on a (semi-)rural police station. It seems a particularly telling cultural indicator that so resolutely urban a genre as a 'cop show' should be placed in such a setting, and that urban audiences should valorise it. Nevertheless, as with other locally made light drama series, such as *Country GP*, there *was* an overseas precedent in the form of a Scottish series called *Sutherland's Law*. As their titles suggest, there was a clear line of descent from *Sutherland's Law* to *Mortimer's Patch*.

For present purposes, however, what is of relevance is the contrast between *Mortimer's Patch* and a subsequent city-based police drama series called *Shark in the Park*. Both of these local series employ the conventions of realism, but both rest upon a fictional conception of the social order. The methodological significance of these programmes does not therefore derive from their relation to some purportedly real conception of New Zealand, but from the system of internal differences revealed by their relation to one another and to their precursors from overseas. Such a comparison provides an opportunity to explore the pressures exerted on the traditional cultural construction of community when it is transposed to a contemporary urban location. Reading the programmes in this way makes of them a kind of cultural tracer, a condensate of those shifts in social consciousness which they are understood as both obliquely signalling and incrementally shaping. Moreover, police dramas are characteristically 'communities to order', texts which permit the rhetorical exploration of the relation between state power and the modes of control characteristic of civil society.

Mortimer's Patch was based on the presumption that there was the potential for tension, but no radical break, between community and police in securing the maintenance of social order. Police authority was exercised by an irascible, aging Pakeha male police inspector (Mortimer) but this was characteristically tempered and regulated by an aging Maori male police sergeant. The latter was presented as more attuned to communal sentiment than was his superior, more mindful of it as a crucial source of social control and therefore more willing to take it into account in deciding on a course of action. He knowingly and laconically attempted to negotiate and mediate the relation between communal authority and state power, between the interpretation of community needs and Mortimer as the (purported) instrument for their achievement. The sergeant was undemonstrative but efficacious, nominally subordinate but effectively occupying the moral centre of the series. Characteristically therefore, his function in the narrative was to be the location of, and repository for, the community's unresolved tensions. In a series in which women were marginalised, he became the proxy for the social and emotional work which women have historically undertaken. In a series in which youth was patronised, he exemplified the wisdom of an older generation rather than the arbitrariness of its power. His role also straddled the distinctions between superior and subordinate, between civil society and state bureaucracy, between Maori communality and European instrumentality; he routinely undertook a form of brokerage in which viewers could at once recognise the divisions of class and ethnicity *and* their accommodation. It was, therefore, both possible and tempting to see the fictional relation between sergeant, authoritarian inspector and local community as going beyond the coded dramatisation of real social tensions. It also offered a reassuring message to a conservative citizenry as to the regulation and management of such problems. For some, it may even have offered confirmation of their tacit understanding of the political relation which they (believed that they) had with their favourite prime minister (Sir Robert Muldoon).

What was therefore signified in the series was the integrating and controlling presence of an imagined *rural* community, and yet what this setting sanctioned was the simultaneous enactment *and containment* of the problems and anxieties of an overwhelmingly *urban* audience. Therein lay the basis of its popular and critical appeal.

Like *Mortimer's Patch*, the conventions and format of the urban-based *Shark in the Park* depends and draws upon a British model. Successful enough to go into a second series, the programme's general conception is clearly indebted to the English police drama *The Bill*, along with echoes of *Softly Softly, Task Force*. Yet on occasion what is also displayed is the influence of American programmes, including the structurally more complex (and visually more accomplished) *Hill Street Blues*. For example, the images which introduce each episode of the series are of downtown office buildings, motorways and fast-moving traffic. They signal that the series is located firmly in the heart of New Zealand's capital city and in the social and material circumstances of the present. In fact, the opening shot explicitly marks the movement away from a rural setting. The camera pans up and back from a green hillside to reveal the city below. A series of jump cuts show various police officers in action and introduces the ten or twelve characters around whom the episodes are organised. As this description implies, the actors and images are local, but in overall realisation the introduction depends upon a structure that has been made familiar by American programmes. Rapid cutting, upbeat music, dramatic camera angles and urban imagery are combined in what seems designed to be a lyrical evocation of the pace, energy and excitement of the city, and the police as its custodians.

Yet this notion of the city as idea and image does not extend into the substantive text of the programme. Within any one episode, the urban setting may sometimes provide for a direct dramatisation of social conflicts—a protest inside a social welfare office, a bomb threat against a refuge for battered women. For the most part, however, the city functions as no more than an impersonal backcloth of streets, business premises, bars and motels. In the series as a whole, the effective locus of community is the pattern of relationships amongst the police themselves, a fusion of bureaucratic organisation, occupational community and social order. The ensemble format of *Shark in the Park* therefore permits the ten or so main characters to engage in what is, at times, a somewhat didactic exploration of the social divisions of age, gender, ethnicity and class, but this is always within an overarching system of control.

Both *The Bill* in the UK and *Hill Street Blues* in the US were, of course, distinguished by their own distinctive presentation of those same divisions. While each clearly exemplified local specificities, between them they have, in effect, defined the general terms under which the police/ urban community relation might be signified. *Shark in the Park's* somewhat equivocal relation to such predecessors is therefore particularly instructive. On the one hand, there is little sense, as there is in *The Bill's* evocation of London's East End, of how social divisions relate to and are grounded in, any wider community. But neither is there the explicit repudiation, as in *Hill Street Blues*, of the notion of a larger community (having even a residual role) as an integrative force. What surged and swarmed through *Hill Street's* densely plotted narratives was an overridingly powerful sense of the city as a place of unproductive *disorder*; the series dramatically portrayed the social and individual costs of institutional failures, failures which both generated and threatened occupational loyalties and communal sentiment amongst the police themselves. *Shark in the Park* borrows from both programmes, but nowhere does it approach capturing a local equivalent of their respective (and contrasting) evocations of urbanism. This seems to me explicable not just as a purely technical shortcoming deriving from budgetary constraints, unevenness in scripting or the limitations of the actors (and thus, in principle, capable of correction). It derives from the difficulty of interpreting a pattern of urban living, whose spatial and material organisation has (as we have seen) more affinities with the USA than with Britain, through cultural categories and assumptions which complexly reflect and refract (as we have seen) a predominantly British legacy. In the rural context of *Mortimer's Patch* an attenuated (and at times critical) version of English pastoral could productively confront a representation (obliquely) invested with a sense of Maori communality by actor Don Selwyn. In *Shark in the Park* neither tradition can be made to play.

In *Mortimer's Patch* narrative resolution depended upon the reconciliation of state authority and community control. In *Shark in the Park* there is a shift in the locus of community towards the police themselves, and this is accompanied by a shift in the pattern of presiding authority. Inspector 'Sharky' Finn (to whom the series title refers) is more benign than Mortimer, less reliant upon the traditional props of bluster and cunning, more attuned to the orthodox homilies of textbooks on management, less wayward (and dramatically much less interesting). His power is more obviously positional than personal, more clearly derived from his location within a bureaucratic structure.

It is precisely the transition to a city milieu which makes some kind of impersonal, rule-based authority system a practical necessity. But in the absence of any complementary or countervailing pattern of community control, it is as if bureaucracy itself must be presented as somehow communal if it is to be made culturally 'safe' and acceptable. For viewers attuned to the conventions of contemporary police dramas, however, this sounds, and looks like, a fantasy fit only for management consultants. By comparison, Inspector Mortimer was a renegade of sorts, a kind of rural Dirty Harry who fired off words instead of bullets.[9] The point is that notwithstanding its rural setting, *Mortimer's Patch* had in this respect been right in line with the cop-show tradition. At its most sophisticated the genre allows for that measured ambivalence towards bureaucracy and its hierarchies that is exhibited by post-liberal, post-feminist police captain Frank Furillo of *Hill Street Blues* (cf. Gitlin 1983, pp.310-12). In *Shark in the Park* there is, however, no equivalent to the intractability of

Furillo's moral dilemmas, nor of his continual struggle to negotiate and hold small areas of moral space for him and his. In the New Zealand series there are too few signals of authority as contingent; of the stressful indeterminacy and fluidity of decision-making under pressure; of an occupational community constructed against, or in spite of, bureaucratic authority rather than in accordance with it. In short, it is culturally timid; too much a training manual, too little a drama; city-based but without city-sense. In this respect it fares badly when compared, for example, with the (purportedly less serious and certainly more salacious) evening soap opera *Gloss*.

In a nation whose citizens are highly mobile, nomadic, consumerist, privatised and urban, images of a more stable, less instrumental, imagined rural community continue to flourish. It might therefore seem that their appeal is precisely that they contradict lived experience whilst acting to reconcile New Zealanders to it. But as the imaginative use and reworking of such film genres as the western has demonstrated, the physical setting of cultural productions seems less pertinent than the kind of preoccupations they permit. What, for example, could be more urban in this sense (or more urbane), than the small town of *Twin Peaks*? Locally this point is demonstrated by discernible differences of pace, mood and mode of address as between the received rural nostalgia characteristic of New Zealand's fully urbanised dominant media culture and that overriding sense of loss which is forcefully conveyed by such recent Maori portrayals of the rural as the fiction of Patricia Grace or Barry Barclay's film *Ngati*. The social division between Maori and Pakeha within the city is expressed through a differential construction of country, through an alternate conception of the divisions between country and city, and thus by implication through a different understanding of the city itself. This suggests that there is nothing accidental about the absence of an explicit, cohesive image of the city in *Shark in the Park*. It does no more than correspond to the explicit absence of social cohesion in practice.

The associated cultural anxieties may also help to explain why *Shark in the Park* seems so constrained. Although its ensemble format allows for a much wider social range than did *Mortimer's Patch*, there is actually less tolerance for difference, disorder, and waywardness in the conduct of its principals. Social categories are dutifully presented rather than effectively represented. The associated social divisions are therefore severely muted; (police) behaviour appears as either more inhibited or more subject to control than in the semi-rural setting of the earlier programme. In consequence, *Shark in the Park* forecloses on the kind of wider cultural sense that is manifestly at work in *Hill Street*'s conscious courting of the absurd, or in the incipient class conflict which seethes through *The Bill*.

Mortimer's Patch did it better. Just as the very concept of 'middle New Zealand' was finally fracturing under the combined impact of the economic, political and social transformations of the 1980s, so the series succeeded in registering, even articulating, something of its frustrations and ambivalences. That cultural moment has now clearly passed. With it has gone the very feasibility of attempting to embody and contain its dilemmas within that narrow social space which Mortimer signified— middle-aged, middle-class, Pakeha male in authority but with an authority problem. This contradictory construction of authority could be made to speak to concerns which went beyond the specifics of Mortimer's social location. One of the cultural legacies of New Zealand's continually interventionist state has been to make its citizens both effectively dependent upon bureaucratic authority and resentful of it. Mortimer is of interest, not just because he both resisted and benefited from such authority, but because notwithstanding the consequences in any given episode, the *overall* narrative effect of the series was to approvingly sanction such resistance as an indication of character.

By comparison with Inspector Finn, Mortimer was therefore 'a bit of a dag', not quite domesticated, a larrikin in a suit. The cultural import of this is that the character was able to tap into a well-worn (and deeply sentimental) theme in the popular mythology of the New Zealand male, that of 'the good keen man', suspicious of emotional and material attachments, tenderness, modernity and cities. The definitive model and limiting case for this cultural tendency is New Zealand's best-selling author, the rural nomad Barry Crump.[10] Since the mid-1980s Crump has also been the central character in a very popular series of television commercials for Toyota's range of small pickup trucks. As a vehicle that is equally at home in both country and city, the pickup truck brings these locations closer together—not just physically, but also semiotically. Toyota's advertising campaign is clearly informed by a recognition of the marketing prospects opened up by this principle. The result is a commercially induced attempt to (re)negotiate the relation between the rural and the urban. These commercials therefore offer an appropriate final example through which some of the threads of this chapter can be drawn together.

Ever since they first appeared, the Toyota/Crump commercials have constructed the contrast between country and city around the relation between Crump (as the principal character) and actor Lloyd Scott. The diminutive Scott plays an urban-based, white-collar worker, whose loquacious naivety, appearance and sentiments are the object of Crump's wry amusement. The latter's sardonic style extends to his debunking of Scott's gushing and overenthusiastic product promotion at the beginning of the commercial. Thus in one case Crump pats the body of a Toyota Hilux twincab and remarks, 'What happened here, Scotty, did the robot hiccup on you?' (The commercial subsequently vindicates the vehicle of course, but visually rather than verbally.) As this implies, the commercials are played for laughs. They consist, for the most part, of the sanguine and laconic Crump (as driver) and the initially apprehensive and subsequently terrified Scott (as passenger) hurtling at high speed along bush-clad country tracks, or climbing impossibly steep inclines in open country, or driving off cliffs in hill-country backblocks.

The popularity and persistence of this theme over several years requires explanation. One way of getting leverage on this question is by way of an early Toyota/Crump commercial which was shown only twice before being withdrawn at the request of the authorities. Much discussed when screened (in the mid-1980s), and much missed when dumped, it survives only as a folk memory (and on the videotape files of the odd academic). Like the others, it features Crump, Scott and a Toyota pickup, but this time in an urban location. Crump has reluctantly come to town for a mate's wedding and he looks distinctly ill at ease in a suit. The pickup speeds through city streets in a hair-raising fashion, but in the changed setting the protagonists' roles are also reversed. The matter-of-fact driver is now Scott, and it is Crump who becomes the much alarmed passenger. Possible models for such scenes reach as far back as Keystone Kops films, but in this instance the more proximate inspiration was probably the Wellington car chase sequence in a local 'road movie' called *Goodbye Pork Pie*. The commercial's humour is somewhat lighter in tone, without that bleak, and finally desperate, manic intensity which emerges from the film. In *Goodbye Pork Pie* authority in general and the police in particular, were persistently and explicitly ridiculed; the Toyota commercial was politically more circumspect, the anarchy less determinate in focus, having acquired its impetus from an emphasis on flight (from marriage). The long-running *Goodbye Pork Pie* broke box-office records in

A relaxed Lloyd Scott and an apprehensive Barry Crump in an urban Toyota commercial that was screened only twice.

New Zealand; the Toyota commercial was taken off the air after two showings (on the grounds that it might encourage dangerous driving practices).

This combination of popular appeal and official disapproval is a signal of territory in dispute, an indication that some kind of boundary had been breached. Given that 'dangerous driving practices', in the form of spec-tacular car chases and crashes, are endemic on film and television, why was *this* commercial singled out? In cultural terms, what is it that gets done through such images?[11]

Consider first the question of popularity. As Roger Horrocks (1985, pp.154-5) has noted, *Goodbye Pork Pie* was a popular success but the response to it divided along gender lines. As with the Toyota commer-cials, the appeal and the orientation was largely to male audiences. In both film and commercials, the 'buddy movie' format of two main char-acters allows for the exploration and negotiation of the distinctions within gender rather than between genders. In *Goodbye Pork Pie* the major axis of differentiation within masculinity was youth/experience, in the Toyota commercials it was risk taking/security. In the latter case what is also mobilised is the tension between the authority and resources of a middle-class job and the traditional construction of masculinity as involving physically demanding work. In general, however, it is noteworthy that such processes of 'internal' differentiation are still more manifest in pro-grammes or films of this type which centre upon women, such as *Cagney and Lacey* or *Thelma and Louise*. This is arguably because they are con-structed against, but begin from, a position of traditional female depend-ence and subordination. As such, they are often about keeping emotions under control in crisis conditions. In the masculine case, by contrast, the narrative function of extreme situations and crisis is, arguably, to override the cultural sanctions against emotional expression, to make it possible.

In a society in which social, cultural, political and economic differ-ences have become more manifest, it is not surprising that the idea of 'the popular' turns out to be problematic. In New Zealand, as elsewhere, the supplementary question is always 'popular with whom?' The proliferation of such differences registers both in the division between country and city and within the cities. Yet the notion that culturally, if not statistically, it is the rural which is the 'real' New Zealand, has proved to be remark-ably resilient. It is therefore not trivial to say that the cultural meaning of rural is 'not urban', but that the cultural use of 'the rural' has effectively been urbanised. It is the locale in which a myth of continuity can engage with the display of difference. It can be read conservatively as the equivalent of damage control, or progressively as a way of edging towards a more open, plural conception of culture. The rural can be made to mean freedom or order; flight or stability; a place to escape the impersonal controls and modes of regulation characteristic of an urban setting, or a place where the regulation of social life occurs largely through spontaneous patterns of community control. But whether the associated imagined community is construed as cripplingly narrow, or maximally inclusive, it nonetheless contains and controls the fissuring and splintering of the idea of a common culture.

Transposition to an urban setting undermines these ambiguities (and the readings from disparate social positions which they permit). What can, in the rural milieu, still be read as the contrast between social order and individual deviance (*Mortimer's Patch*, Toyota's rural commercials) becomes, in the city, the clash of social differences (*Goodbye Pork Pie*, Toyota's urban commercial). The enforcement of formal and impersonal regulations comes to replace, rather than supplement, the interweaving of moral order, social evaluation, rumour and gossip as modes of control. What this signals is, moreover, not just a change in the *means* of control. The very idea of community as the point of moral reference and overarching constraint loses its force, leaving the residue of its hollowed-out shell scattered across the more formal structures of organisation (*Shark in the Park*).

A disorganising and disorderly dynamic, with the market as its engine, is very much at work in *all* of the Crump/Scott/Toyota commercials. Their commonalities of pace, rhythm and structure immediately identify them as products of urbanism and as oriented towards a celebration of freely mobile individuals. On one view it would be surprising if it were otherwise. Advertising is, after all, the official art of capitalism (and therefore has some structural affinities with socialist realism, albeit inspired by a different set of fantasies). But since advertising also has an ideology of its own—selling something/anything, but selling it—its relation to other ideological precepts is a contingent rather than a necessary one. And if, as in New Zealand, the idea of community sells, then community can be sold too. This awareness is not, of course, limited to the advertising industry. The audience also knows it, and advertisers know that they know. In their most recent collaboration Crump and Scott explore how to acknowledge, and to use, the scepticism and resistance which comes with that audience knowledge. It occurs in a type of commercial which is designed not to sell a particular product directly, but rather to establish an association between Toyota's name and valued activities and ideals.

It features Crump (as usual, in bush gear) and Scott (in sailor suit) leading an enthusiastic singalong at a local community hall. The commercial marks Toyota's role as a sponsor of New Zealand's participation in the 1992 America's Cup Challenge in San Diego. The local community is clearly intended to signify the nation as a whole, and at one level the commercial can be read as attempting to generate the kind of enthusiasm and interest associated with a previous America's Cup contest. There are therefore conscious echoes of earlier America's Cup commercials and of New Zealand's Telethon as discussed in Chapter Two. Such intertextuality can, however, be read another way, not least because the commercial deliberately deploys a kind of calculated euphoria, a mood of fabricated excess which edges towards parody. That this is deliberate is made evident in the subdued and laconic coda, itself intertextual. It nods towards the memorable conclusion of a well-known Nilverm commercial, to be discussed in Chapter Four, in which the central figure sips his beer, glances at the viewer and cryptically observes of a cricket-playing small boy who has just bowled underarm, 'He may play for Aussie one day, that little fella'. At the close of the Toyota commercial, Crump gratefully grasps a beer, looks towards the camera, and observes of Scott's euphoric participation in the singalong that, 'He's a danger to shipping, that bloke'. The effect is to put the rest of the commercial in quotation marks, to bracket what has gone before.

It may also remind viewers that when this small man in a sailor suit drives a Toyota pickup in a city street, he is seen as a danger both to traffic and to the authorities. Without community, his energy, enthusiasm and euphoria becomes an unguided missile. And yet this commercial also signals its own fictionality, that its community is imagined. The worldliness of this repudiation of realism is both encouraging and distressing. It is arguably an acknowledgement of audience sophistication. It is also part of that same process of erosion and fragmentation which at once opens up alternatives and undercuts belief in the possibility of a wider community. This does not necessarily mean that community *per se* is absent. It certainly does mean that it appears increasingly crump(led).

Between laconic and euphoric: Barry Crump and Lloyd Scott in Toyota's 1992 America's Cup campaign commercials. →

1 By 1986 there were almost 80,000 farms, around half of which were devoted largely or entirely to either sheep and/or dairy production (NZ Dept of Statistics 1989; pp.518-9). The extremely condensed version of New Zealand's economic development presented in this section derives from an earlier paper on structural change within the New Zealand political economy. See Perry (1992a).

2 There are many similarities to the Australian pattern of urbanism. The most developed theoretical attempt to understand this Australian (and by implication, New Zealand) form is the Castells-inspired account by Pat Mullins (1981a; 1981b).

3 For example, it is worth noting that despite the modest level of per capita income, the number of telephones complements the figures for vehicle ownership. In 1972 there were 458 telephones per 1000 people (fifth highest in the OECD), rising to 648 per 1000 by 1985 (sixth highest in the OECD).

4 Toyota City is the industrial complex some fifty or so kilometres from the centre of Tokyo where Toyota and its hundreds of supplier firms have their base.

5 New car purchasers in Japan are required to produce documentation that they can provide sufficient space for the vehicle to to be parked. Only then can the sale be finalised.

6 Adjudicating between these somewhat stylised theoretical alternatives is *not* the purpose of this chapter. On the contrary, it emphasises an approach to popular culture which consciously foregrounds and replicates the tension between these positions (or, if you will, that is *how* it adjudicates between them, cf. Ryle 1964; pp.15-35, 68 *et seq.*). Popular culture is understood as a means by which ordinary men and women strive to make something of their lives, through whatever resources are available to them. In a consumer society it is expressed in the transformations and uses that they make of images, artifacts and social expectations that are characteristically made for them rather than made by them (cf. Fiske 1989a). What is therefore a structural property and constitutive dilemma of popular culture is that, *at the moment of its making*, it is an enactment of contradictory elements in the social order. This opens up the methodological possibility that the plurality of its determinations can be (indirectly) detected in the kind of cultural images and popular narratives through which meanings circulate.

The existence of ethnic, gender, class and age divisions does, however, mean that the boundaries of 'the popular' will admit of no stable definition. Sometimes it is constructed across such distinctions, sometimes not. Just how such social divisions are constituted, and the associated question of 'whose popular culture?', will therefore admit of no general answer. The popular is simply that cultural location in which such issues are played out (under conditions where the distinction between 'worked through' and 'played out'—i.e. the prioritising of production over consumption as the locus of determinacy—is itself problematic).

7 See the discussion by Lawrence Jones (1989).

8 Compare the conversation between Alice and Humpty Dumpty in Lewis Carroll's *Through the Looking Glass* (1971, p.191): "'That's a great deal to make one word mean,'" Alice said in a thoughtful tone. "'When I make a word do a lot of work like that,'" said Humpty Dumpty, "'I always pay it extra.'"

9 This confers an ironic double meaning on the series title. In (British) police dramas the usual meaning of 'patch' (as in *Mortimer's Patch*) is as a way of talking about a senior police officer's area of territorial jurisdiction. In New Zealand the expression 'patch' also refers to the main symbol and identifying insignia worn by members of motor cycle gangs.

10 *A Good Keen Man* is the title of Crump's best-known work. Total sales of his novels now exceed a million copies.

11 Read one way, this and the other Toyota commercials, even more than the television programmes which they punctuate (or Crump's books), are escapist fantasies serving only to confirm a disjunction between image and experience. Read another, such images may be seen to act as a condensate of feelings and thereby *constitutive* of experience. The first approach privileges the properties of the work, prioritises the system which produces it and prejudges the sentiments of those who consume it. The second approach subordinates the properties of the work to the place it comes to occupy within the culture of the audience; it is this practice which it privileges and this culture which it prioritises. On this latter view, a 'successful' work is one which discursively organises and summarises the emergent sentiments of the audience in ways that the latter can (or can be persuaded to) recognise and value. (Oh, and it may also help to sell Toyota, if not Toyotas.)

Oscillating promiscuously between these two reading strategies is a third. It is more tactical, pragmatic, provisional, less theoretically or epistemologically principled (cf. note 6). In recognising that cultures are resistant to Method, it nonetheless remains mindful of maintaining appearances. Its premiss is that cultural analysis both invites and requires equivocation between an 'internal' and an 'external' reading; between (the uncertain phenomenological adequacy of) a mode of sorting and (the uneven theoretical control of) a method of sorts. It is part fan and part fan; drawn to the warm, sticky pleasures of cultural immersion, and to the cool relief of detachment and distancing. I(t) want(s), that is, what is possible only in language—to eat cake and still have it.

FOUR

Restricted Vision

Images of Australia in New Zealand Television Commercials

The playwright Oscar Wilde once suggested that the British and the Americans had everything in common except language. This was both a very aristocratic and a very British thing to say. It's the kind of sardonic remark one might expect when a threatened sensibility tries to combat— with words as weapons—the ever-more-manifest material superiority and technical virtuosity of another culture. Conversely there seems something characteristically American about the MIT engineering student described by the historian of technology Elting Morison (1962, p.17). He apparently summarised the most famous dramatic work in the English language by suggesting that the trouble with Hamlet was that he had too much feedback on his circuits. Furthermore what was said to be tragic about the play was that its hero operated at only 16.67 per cent efficiency (i.e. about that of an internal combustion engine) because he had one person to kill but actually got rid of six.

With the expansion of the dominion of signs such waywardness may have lost the power to shock but it retains the power to surprise. In this particular case it is the disparity between the linguistic conventions appropriate to the very different disciplines of literary criticism and engineering which makes the interpretation appear so exotic. The coexistence of a variety of different approaches *within* a single discipline is, of course, the chronic condition of sociology. It is therefore one of the conditions for engaging in the sociological craft that its practitioners become worldly wise about the undermining effects of different modes of discourse. Using the same words provides no guarantees of shared understanding. If they prove to be ordered and organised through different discourses, then an agreed agenda, a shared lexicon and a purportedly common subject matter will not produce unifying effects.

The kind of translation problems to which Oscar Wilde and Morison's engineer call attention are at work in our part of the world. The subject of this chapter is one such subversive device. I want to try and make more explicit that pattern of half-hidden assumptions, codes and conventions which govern the imagery and interpretations through which New Zealanders construct—or rather invent—Australia. How we read 'them' does, of course, say something about 'us'. As with the images of New Zealand and New Zealandness investigated in Chapters Two and Three, 'our' images of Australia are related to patterns of social division within this country. My route into this territory is via three television advertisements. All of them were made by New Zealand agencies, and all of them have recently—and, of course, repeatedly—been shown on prime-time television throughout New Zealand. As with the analysis of Telethon, the emphasis is on trying to reconstruct the kind of cultural milieu in which such adverts are not only possible, but also come to be regarded as exemplary, as managing to both summarise and articulate the sentiments of the audience to which they appeal. The focus is thus not so much on the semiotic details of the texts, nor on the context of their production, but rather *between* text and context. More particularly, this methodology involves probing into those aspects of the adverts which might account for their being not merely tolerated by viewers, but actually enjoyed, even cherished, by them.

Two of the adverts make use of rural settings. Chapter Three noted the pervasiveness of rural imagery and themes within a society that is, along with Australia, one of the most urbanised in the world. Such images occur and recur not only in New Zealand adverts but in the locally made programmes which they punctuate, not only in television but in New Zealand films and literature. In Chapter Three the emphasis was on the conflicts and tensions *within* the urban environment, paying particular attention to their representation within a rural milieu and via a rural mythology. In a society distinguished by the statistical dominance of the urban population and the (declining) structural power of the rural sector, there are, in addition, major sources of tension and conflict *between* the urban and the rural. I propose to argue that what these adverts incidentally reveal are the tensions associated with managing the contradictions associated with this latter division. The idea of Australia is both a topic *sui generis* and a resource in this specifically local struggle.

The first rural advert that I propose to discuss was made for an ICI subsidiary called Coopers. It was designed to sell a sheep drench called Nilverm.

The manifest target audience for this advert was, of course, New Zealand farmers. That an urban audience were exposed to it at all is because achieving an adequate coverage of rural areas necessarily involves transmitting to all the urban centres. Thus not only did farmers have no part in producing it but they were not the only people to have watched it. It was, in fact, voted one of the top three television commercials of 1985 by the overwhelmingly urban and middle-class readership of Auckland's *Metro* magazine (1986, p.78). It is this anomalous configuration which provides a point of entry for my reading.

The opening shot of a somewhat ramshackle farm is not only identified by subtitles as being Cullengoral, Australia, but is accompanied on the sound track by the raucous 'laughter' of kookaburras. Nonetheless the opening visuals, with their echoes of a Russell Drysdale painting, and the authentic sound of Australian wildlife, might just admit of a lyrical or affirmative reading, a down-under version of a chocolate-box aesthetic. The sound of distant conversation prefigures the cut to the farm verandah: a newly arrived visitor is introduced by the farmer to the local vet (and one other man) as 'My brother-in-law, over from Kiwiland'. The locals are bedecked in the uniform of Ockerdom, grimy shorts, singlets and working shirts, whereas the new arrival is clothed in a sober shirt and tie and is carrying an equally sober suit jacket.

These visual signals of authority are reinforced when the conversation turns to veterinary matters, and the group moves round to the back of the farmhouse. The visitor alternately interrogates and instructs. The instruction depends upon an invidious contrast (for Australians) between Australian and New Zealand performance with respect to both sheep production and sporting achievement. These two arenas are linked through the colour of the sheep drench. 'Gold?' says the farmer. 'Same colour as those medals we won in L.A.,' responds the visitor, 'but then you wouldn't have seen too many of that colour, would you?'

The pack shot (i.e. the image which identifies the product being advertised) is followed by a brief coda. Like the ad's opening sequence it might just be read as picturesque.

In the background is an ancient, rusting and immobile farm truck; in the foreground two young boys are playing cricket. The bowler, clad in Australia's national colours (and gumboots) sends down an underarm delivery. 'Oh, Trevor,' shouts the other boy in exasperation. Cut to a shot of the New Zealander together with one of the women at the farm (and who might just be intended to be his sister). He laconically observes, 'He could play for Aussie one day, that little fella'. The woman half smiles, and then glances at the visitor. She, unlike the viewer, cannot see the self-satisfied look on his face. The mocking sound of kookaburras is heard once more. Fade out.

All such adverts presuppose visual literacy. Perhaps one reason why small children lock into them is that they are particularly instructive in this respect. A crucial point about the Nilverm ad, however, is that it does not only and not simply presuppose a knowing audience. It also flatters them, grants them recognition for being insiders. It presumes that they are familiar with, and care about sport as an expression of national identity; that they are cosmopolitan enough to know what 'L.A.' means; that they are aware of the relative gold medal tallies of Australia and New Zealand at the 1984 Olympics; and that they are acquainted with, and were exasperated by, Australian Trevor Chappell's underarm ball at the end of a tightly contested cricket match between the two countries.

The audience is presumed to be knowing in a more general sense. They are expected to be aware of the disparity between frontal facade and operational practice, and to relish the unmasking of the former. Thus the call of the kookaburra gives way to the sound of flies, and the possibly picturesque—or at least 'authentic'—gives way to the manifestly shoddy. This is not only clearly signalled verbally, 'Keeps it hidden, does he?', but also visually in the movement from the front of the farmhouse to the back. It's an exposure that is almost indecent. Indeed the ad was the subject of formal complaints to the Race Relations Conciliator, on the grounds that it discriminated against Australians. The judgement of the Conciliator's Office was a publicist's delight. Their conclusion was that there was no case to answer. After all, the advert *was* filmed at Cullengoral, there *are* farms like the one depicted, and they *do* get three sheep to the acre. Furthermore, all of the actors involved, including the visitor, were Australians.

This is a judgement which attends only to what might be called the surface of the commercial as a text. It is both too literal and too literary an interpretation for our purposes. I have already pointed out the way in

Drenched with sarcasm: Australian sheep-farmers and the Nilverm commercial. →

Cullengoral, Australia

which the content of this advert moves and works in the contrast between front and back, between facade and substance. These distinctions also apply to its *form*. Its effects are achieved through the interaction of spoken word and visual image, of what is said, the way it's said, and how it's shown. This is most explicit in the coda, in which only the camera is privy to both the visitor's look of self-satisfaction and to the woman's querulous half-smile. It is this combination, together with the local cultural knowledge which the viewer must bring to bear, which gives the spoken words their meaning, and allows for the encoded message to be understood. Throughout the ad the viewer is drawn into such conspiracies: the visitor's laconic one-liners are always for the camera rather than for his hosts. It is therefore in an aesthetic, rather than a judicial sense, that the charge of indecent exposure might be made to stick. This is an advert which publicly plays with itself. It is not surprising that the farm wife didn't know whether to laugh or not.

The Office of the Race Relations Conciliator was also silent about the advert's ideology, the way in which it strives to embody a more general cultural statement about Australia and Australians in and through its specificities. A central theme of the ad is trans-tasman competition; the terrain on which it is purportedly played out is sport and farming, locations in which New Zealand is indeed competitive. But in this microcosm it is conversation itself which is the locus of competition, and in this contest the visitor enjoys not just a sporting chance but a monopoly of winning lines. From the beginning both green and gold are set to come under the control of the New Zealander—as in the lush green pasture that is evident from the photograph of New Zealand sheep which he shows to his hosts. It is left to the Australian farmer to verbalise what is visually apparent, i.e. New Zealand superiority ('Now that's what I call a sheep') and then to be mocked for saying so ('You don't miss much, do you?'). The correlate of monopoly is, of course, appropriation—no wonder that in thirty seconds the visitor partakes of a beer, a sausage, and a sandwich—all without a word of thanks. In the popular culture of New Zealand males such boorishness is half-admired, both as an expression of that famous Aussie maxim 'no bullshit' and as a sign of strength. It is seen as characteristic of home-grown property millionaires and—as a recent McNair (1986, pp.37–38) survey indicates—of Australian visitors. The ad therefore deliberately inverts what is perceived to be the conventional pattern of hospitality.

In this ad the women are also 'round the back', they have little presence and no voice; we glimpse the performance of domestic tasks—the rest is silence. But one of those women is the visitor's sister and it is this status which can be made to speak. For it is what makes the provision of hospitality an obligation and all that verbal competition a possibility. The women have the obligations and the men have the possibilities. I've argued that this ad articulates the typical concerns and sense of resentment felt by the inhabitants of a small country about their relations with a much larger and more powerful neighbour. What is also typical is that the attendant nationalist sentiment is orchestrated for the commercial benefit of a transnational corporation. But this seems to me insufficient to account for its appeal to an urban audience. My suggestion is that what the Australian location both sanctions and conceals is the antipathy of city dwellers towards the farm sector. This is an implicit meaning rather than a manifest intention. For as I will eventually argue, what the idea of 'Australia' is most likely to invoke for most New Zealanders is not the outback nor the sheep station but the city.

As a necessary preamble to that claim, I want to talk about another popular New Zealand ad which has a rural setting, this time a wholly indigenous one. This provides an opportunity to examine the cultural effects which flow from the city/country distinction when they are unmediated by the kind of nationalist feelings to which the Nilverm ad appeals. This second ad was made by Colenso for Apple Computers, and the analysis which follows extends and amends an earlier one by Ian Carter and myself (Carter & Perry 1987).

The opening shots are of the bar of a country hotel. Apart from a barmaid, and one table of women sitting together, the clientele is exclusively male. The men are wearing working clothes. The encoded mood is of weariness, of lives used up. Apart from the sound of a racetrack commentary in the background, the only animation comes from a Tom Selleck look-alike; an All Black lock in his gardening gear. He tries to start a conversation with a fellow drinker, throwing out laconic one-liners while munching fistfuls of peanuts. 'Had to put the dog down.' No response. 'The missus shot through with the bloke down the road.' Still no response. In keeping with the conventions of Kiwi masculinity, he keeps his motives out of his speech. For the camera's benefit, however, they are conspicuously displayed on his face. More intense facial anticipation. 'Bought a computer.' Pandemonium in the pub. Cut to the pub

Learning how to hack it: Apple's commercial for computers on the farm.

car park, where his mate disparages the farmer's purchase with a single word 'Computer!' Cut to a long focus, head-on shot, as the entire male clientele rides assorted machinery in an anarchic charge to the farm to view this new marvel. It looks like a chase scene from the Keystone Kops or *Bonnie and Clyde*, or, to bring it closer to home, a clip from *Goodbye Pork Pie*. Cut to the poorly lit farm barn, where (incongruously) the Apple PC is kept. The men edge towards the machine. 'It looks harmless enough,' says an unidentified voice. 'Have you got *Deep Throat?*' asks another, clearly identified as the farmer's best mate. Appreciative male guffaws. Initial fear is dissipated as the proud owner shows the computer's marvellous abilities. Quick cuts between shots of the VDU screen and admiring faces lead to the scene's climax. The best mate leans forward and stares intently at the screen display. 'Great subsidy!' he breathes. The farmer looks pleased, then claps his hands over his mate's mouth: 'Oh, you're not supposed to see (say?) that.' Cut to a coda as the inspecting party breaks up. 'Hydatids, was it?' asks the mate. 'Tractor' comes the farmer's reply. We have returned to the opening sequence both in content (how the dog died) and in style (laconic understatement). The prevailing rules of conduct, briefly disturbed by the men's unwontedly animated admiration for the new purchase, have been re-established.

When this ad was first shown in the second half of 1984, it shared advertising time with another one, made for the same company by the same agency, but having an office setting and an urban location. This suggests that it may have been intended, either in whole or in part, to be a 'farming-as-a-business' ad. But whereas it endured well into the second half of 1985, its urban counterpart was taken off New Zealand television screens very much earlier. Yet if the prime target audience was indeed farmers, then from the outset they were unlikely to see that climactic crack about subsidies as either endearing or funny. And by the time the ad dropped from sight it had become bitterly ironic, as New Zealand farmers, like their Australian counterparts, began to take to the streets in order to advertise their problems in a very different way.

Whatever the intention, what the ad shows is that it was produced by urbanites and appeals to city-based audiences. It also appeals to men. The ad talks to business owners and executives threatened by competition, by doubts about their competence in the face of new technology, by novel challenges to patriarchal attitudes. They are reassured on all three counts. For if the hero's combination of terse speech and a boyish animated expression signals a good Kiwi joker, it also suggests that he may not be *quite* as bright as the potential purchaser of an Apple PC. But if *he* can hack it . . . And although there may be women in the public bar, there are none in the barn. The penetration of some traditional male enclaves is balanced by the creation of new bastions of male power where boys can do anything, including showing pornographic videos. The traditional hardware of patriarchy is seen in the race to the farm, and once there its new software is revealed. Perhaps the reason why the computer is kept in the barn is so that the house can remain the locale for women's work. No wonder the missus shot through.

The way in which this is accomplished is very subtle. Partly it has to do with lighting, which bounces off European painterly canons. Everything is muted, with brown the dominant tone. The pub scene is chiaroscuro, Rembrandt with gumboots, backlit by the late afternoon sun. The light is fading as the men race to the farm. Once there, light is needed in the barn. The new machine is illuminated by a single light bulb (McLuhan's pure information); the screen's etherial green glow lights up the admiring faces in an update of conventional representations of the Nativity, in which technological shepherds watch their flicks by night— the adoration of the cagey.

The coda takes place late in the evening. It points up a motif as central to this ad as the front/back distinction was to the Nilverm one. Here the contrast is between the onset of darkness and the possibility of light; between defeat and exhaustion in which death (of a dog) and dissolution (of a marriage) are routine, and a technological promise of enlightenment. But that enlightenment is user-friendly—it reinforces existing social relations.

The Apple ad offers a conventional rural setting, but not a conventional rural iconography. There is no celebration of free landscape, no pastoral lyricism, not even much in the way of daylight. Instead what we are shown are dimly lit interiors, a vehicular free-for-all, and the night. It is by way of this rather distinctive ambience that the ad gives expression to a form of dark comedy for which there are precedents not only in New Zealand literature, but more recently in New Zealand films.

I suggested earlier that the race to the barn echoed scenes in the locally made film *Goodbye Pork Pie*. Both its popularity and its influence on commercials were noted in Chapter Three. It has been described as a 'road movie with menaces', an apposite way of conveying its distinctive pattern of narrative development. What begins as the film's near slapstick style is progressively undercut by a growing feeling of desperation and a heightened sense of threat. Although this conception of the comic was not based on a pre-existing story, it is represented in New Zealand literature, particularly in the work of Ronald Hugh Morrieson, and is now routinely referred to as 'Taranaki gothic'. New Zealand film-makers—and audiences—seem particularly drawn to his work; three of his four books have been made into full-length features. As critics have noted, Morrieson uses both the western (*Came a Hot Friday*) and the thriller (*The Scarecrow*) as models for his fiction. The film version of *The Scarecrow* came out before the Apple ad and may well have influenced it. In cinematic terms, the thriller is the city's genre. *The Scarecrow*, however, is actually set in a small New Zealand town in the 1950s. Thus the film was not a genre movie in the sense of being responsive to the disciplines associated with that term. Nonetheless it depended, like the Apple commercial, on the selective appropriation of some of the conventions of genre. That film and ad share the same look is because each edges towards an urban iconography in a rural setting.

The final ad that I'm going to discuss is again about Australia. It was made for Air New Zealand by Dobbs Wiggin McCann-Erickson.

In this ad a veritable smorgasbord of images is presented in rapid succession, in its thirty seconds of running time there are more than forty cuts. The ad begins with images of water sports and beach life, cutting quickly between shots of men and women, adults and children, individuals and groups. These give way to cityscapes, and urban night life, which in turn are punctuated by somewhat different beach shots, a couple of outback and rural images and a view of an Air New Zealand 747 in flight. The ad concludes with a lingering shot of an aircraft's cabin complete with smiling air hostess.

The accompanying sound track is a jingle whose opening lines are 'Australia's gotta lotta go, whatta lotta go it's got' and which closes with the suggestion that 'Australia's got the lot'.

It is this jingle which integrates the ad and provides its narrative line. The cutting is so fast that, without cues from the sound track, a linear reading of the visual imagery would require several viewings. As it is the most easily recalled scenes are those which contain little internal movement—such as a view of Sydney's skyline, a bikini-clad torso and a glimpse of a drag show. A hint of prurience combines with that process of commodification which is a defining characteristic of adverts. And like all adverts this one both orchestrates desire and points to how it can be met. The ad targets in on a general sense of incompleteness, that chronic psychological condition which a market society strives to induce. It presupposes an absence and it offers consumerism's utopian promise. But because it constructs Australia as a country of the New Zealand mind, it also speaks to the specificities of New Zealand as a post-colonial society. Thus the general psychological concerns which a market society promotes are fused with specifically local anxieties deriving from semi-peripheral status. The ad not only posits the universal experience of relative deprivation—the sense that some*one* else is better off—but also implies marginality—that the centre is some*where* else. It's not simply that Australia's 'gotta lotta go': in the course of the ad it becomes the definite article—it's 'got the lot'.

Just as the sheer number of images signals choice, diversity and opportunity, so too does the pace and rhythm of the ad carry a message of its own. It serves as a formal analogy for the tempo of modernity and city life. This interacts with the diverse content so as to collapse locations dispersed in space into the allocation of time. Thus as a definition of Australia the very form of the ad signals not the distances and the emptiness of the interior but the density of the cities.

The social range of this ad's opening shots reveals that women are part of the target audience. But with the transition from the diversity of the potential clientele to the diversity of Australia the commodification becomes more manifest. Consider, for example, that image of a bikini-clad young woman lying on an air-bed. It's a pin-up style shot of a peculiarly modern type—one which a blanket criticism of all such images cannot isolate. The blanket objection to pin-ups is that they construe women as sex objects; considered semiotically the point is that their meaning is not just denotative but connotative. They stand in for, but have a determinate connection with, the pleasure that men everywhere take in looking at women's bodies. The problem is not the pleasure, but its relation to consent and its mediation under modern conditions. The traditional pin-up is at one remove from the complexities—and the chance of shared pleasure—associated with the actual relationships between men and women. But what the traditional pin-up does leave open is the possibility of movement from a subject/object to a subject/subject relation. What distinguishes the body shot under discussion is that it goes much further in attenuating the relation between male desire and the mutuality of pleasure. First of all, we see the woman as if she does not see us; erotic appeal is conceptually divorced from consent *within* the image itself. Second, when first we see her, she is faceless by design; the shot cuts the woman up, objectifying desire in terms of the parts of her body. By the standards of some magazine adverts it is, of course, a modest, even a conservative image.[1] Nonetheless we can say that in the selling of Australia, fetishism becomes a commodity. In such a context, the lingering image of a smiling air hostess seems to belong to another, earlier time and to another place—namely, New Zealand. It might even be read as a working woman making the best of a bad job—domestic service in a changed context. It seems churlish to see it as a metaphor for inauthenticity, when the deceit lies in the imputation of glamour.

In focusing on the details of each advert, my concern has been to establish what each can be made to reveal. I want to conclude by commenting briefly on the uniformities of gender, class and nation which underpin and condition the differences between them. The images of women as models of domestic virtue, as threats to mateship, and as toys for the boys, represent different points along the axis of patriarchy in a market society, whereas the celebration of the urban and the critique of the rural moves at the intersection of class and nation. The social grouping which this combination of ads is produced by, and tends to select for, consists of compradors;[2] male, urban, middle-class New Zealanders oriented towards overseas metropolitan centres and antipathetic to agrarian petty-commodity producers. The more of those social categories one occupies, and the more of those attitudes one shares, the greater the appeal of these ads. The ads themselves are a kind of peripheral vision; refracted images of New Zealand's changing web of dependencies. The view from the centre looks rather different of course, as in the American tendency to filter perception of Australia through the metaphor and mythology of the frontier. Or at least, that's how Americans interpret Australian movies, notably *Crocodile Dundee*. For New Zealanders by contrast, Australia is only 'way out west' geographically. Structurally and culturally it is as much 'back east' as the United States itself.

My suggestion then, is that these ads are both inadvertent signals of the economic and social location of comprador strategies and implicit measures of the ideology which justifies them. This ideology works to restrict the imagery through which both Australia and New Zealand are invented. It is with some style and imagination that both countries are sold to us—but both are necessarily sold short.

1 Since this was written this strategy has been deployed in other locally made television commercials.
2 Comprador is a term widely employed in development studies to refer to that indigenous section of the middle class in an economically dependent country whose activities serve to consolidate the interests of overseas metropolitan centres.

FIVE

Black to the Future

A methodological problem has been lurking in the margins and notes of previous chapters. Up until this point my emphasis has been on television programmes and advertisements as a cultural tracer of the characteristics of the wider society. Despite some equivocation, the overriding tendency has been to treat such texts as relatively inert materials, as available for scrutiny and inspection through a sociological lens. This gives priority to sociology as an active *form of knowledge* and constructs the texts as the passive *objects of that knowledge*. The result is that despite having proposed in Chapter One that the fictional notion of 'the real New Zealand' be prohibited from entering by the front gate, in subsequent chapters a specifically sociological version of it may nevertheless have tended to sneak (or be smuggled back) in through the rear door. In effect, sociology became the text of texts, providing the ultimate point of reference and the authoritative interpretation of what the others all 'really' mean.

But sociology does not enjoy any such uniquely privileged position in relation to 'the real'. It too is a particular mode of representation, an aspect of culture like any other, subject to its own narrative conventions, its own (contested) notions of good practice, and its own institutional preconditions and forms of social and material support. Yet any author must, of course, use *some* language and therefore presume *some* factors as simply given. In this chapter I make use of a Steinlager All Blacks commercial to signal something of the changes in cultural conditions and the difficulties that they present for sociology's more traditional modes of representation. More particularly, I try to take account of how the texts of television and advertising constitute a phenomenologically distinct cultural reality, a different cultural language. They have transformed not just the cultural landscape, but also how it must be navigated and how it might be (provisionally) mapped. The dilemma is one which I have summarised elsewhere as:

> . . . whether to describe change through a language which itself is un-changing or whether to convey change directly through changes in the very language of description. The choice is between continuity of communication and descriptive adequacy. A familiar form of words maintains communication but fails as description (because the changed reality evades the familiar linguistic categories) whereas the unfamiliar mode of expression may better capture the new situation but fail as communication. . . . It isn't sufficient to say that stable verities have become galloping variables; it must also be shown. Received categories and concepts seem inadequate to the task of understanding such a change precisely because the transformation extends to include them. (Perry 1992b, p.236)

So much for the story so far. Now read on . . .

Academic p(a)role bored? Lang(u)e for something different? Then why not sign up for *The Text Offensive*, a late, late game show which offers a predominantly literary exploration of a predominantly visual medium. This programme is brought to you by the studio which was earlier responsible for 'Cinderella and the Silver Mercedes'. Ready to enter the labyrinth? Remember, there are no strings attached. But first, this pause for network identification . . .

• • •

Pierre Macherey (1978, p.16) once suggested that literary criticism could be summed up as a note in the margin of the book which reads 'could do better'. Both the signs and the times have changed since then. It is not just that contemporary critical practice cannot any longer take for granted that literature occupies a privileged position in relation to other forms of representation. It is also that the tradition of interpreting texts has given way to a strategy of interrupting them (cf. Silverman & Torode 1980). As a result, a text is nowadays somewhat less likely to be read as a *pre*text, i.e. in terms of its deviation from some e(x)ternal standard of aesthetic purity or political correctness. As always, (x) marks the spot, but it now signals the location of a deliberate mistake, or the presence of an alien brand, or the kiss of a promiscuous signifier, rather than the site of buried treasure.

Although some of pretext's long list of disappointed lovers have turned to context for consolation, they too have failed to find satisfaction. An emphasis on the context in which texts are produced offers a corrective to any assumption that they are the product of immaculate conception. There is an increased receptivity to such sociological approaches, but a continuing resistance to that kind of sociological reductionism through which texts are not so much read, as read off, from the conditions of their production. The assumption of ideological conspiracy is as unsatisfactory as the assumption of immaculate conception. Such preordained readings can always be made to work—they cannot, however, be made to play (cf. Perry 1993). Yet play is not the opposite of seriousness, but rather its essential accomplice.[1] Our willingness to play, and the play of the text on us, is the condition of that familiarity with the body of the text on which our pleasure depends. Having ushered novelty into the wor(l)d, that body is replete with the signs of life. And because it lies between the death of the author and the birth of the reader, it is also the custodian of polyvalent possibilities.

Texts thus remain resolutely Other in relation to the overtures of sociology. Texts are both a source and a site of pleasure/discovery/exasperation/argument. Inasmuch as sociology rests upon a determination to control that waywardness, then it can only promise a seduction which deserves to be repudiated, and only aspire to a consummation which is destined to be endlessly deferred. Texts are all for(e)play. They therefore require lovers, but the principles which guide the resulting relation are the indeterminacies of flirtation. What better topic for identifying the basis of such textual pleasures than the practice of *opus interruptus*? What better subject for investigating such a strategy of interruption than television commercials? And what better subject for the exploration of masculine fantasies than a beer commercial devoted to the All Blacks?

And now, back to the future . . .

• • •

Our first item is a golden oldie, remastered and recycled for today's audiences: Raymond Williams's classic production of *Miami Splice*.

One night in Miami, still dazed from a week on an Atlantic liner, I began watching a film (on television) and at first had some difficulty in adjusting to a much greater frequency of commercial 'breaks'. Yet this was a minor problem compared to what eventually happened. Two other films, which were due to be shown on the same channel on other nights, began to be inserted as trailers. A crime in San Francisco (the subject of the original film) began to operate in an extraordinary counterpoint not only with the deodorant and cereal commercials but with a romance in Paris and the eruption of a prehistoric monster who laid waste New York . . . Even in British commercial television there is a visual signal— the residual sign of an interval—before and after the commercial sequences, and 'programme' trailers only occur between programmes. Here there was something quite different, since the transitions from film to commercial and from film A to films B and C were in effect unmarked. There is in any case enough similarity between certain kinds of films, and between several kinds of film and the situation commercials which often consciously imitate them, to make a sequence of this kind a very difficult experience to interpret. I can still not be sure what I took from that whole flow. I believe I registered some incidents as happening in the wrong film, and some characters in the commercials as involved in the film episodes, in what came to seem—for all the occasional bizarre disparities—a single irresponsible flow of images and feelings. (Williams 1974, pp. 91–92)

• • •

The experience which Williams describes (and the influential account of television's distinctive 'flow' to which it gave rise) dramatises a methodological issue which traditional forms of criticism have treated as unproblematic, i.e. the question of what constitutes the television text. The difficulty here goes beyond the kind of distinction that has been made, for example, between 'literature' and a given book, or between 'cinema' and a particular film (cf. Metz 1982); between the material specificity of this novel or that movie, and the system which organises its realisation. The predominance of the serial form on television; the very notion of an evening's viewing; the bewilderment induced if you watch only *one* episode of a midday soap; the temporal scheduling of programme types; the secular litany of channel identification, forthcoming attractions and the commercials; all these combine to interrogate the notion of a single programme as the modal television text. The fragment, the schedule and the series have each been claimed as the crucial unit of enquiry. My own interest is the methodological and critical possibilities which are opened up by assigning modality to the commercials. They are the hook on which the aforementioned inventory of characteristics can be said to hang. And although the efficacy of the hook depends upon the exoticism of its surrounding lures, it is a hook which nevertheless governs the shapes those lures may take. An incidental theme of Chapter Six is that it is in this way that the commercials' presence effectively looms over those locations (such as the BBC or PBS) from which they are formally absent.

In the United States the 1987 price of screening a thirty-second commercial on *The Cosby Show* was $US440,000. A spot during the Superbowl would have required an outlay of perhaps $US1 million (Ewen 1989). In New Zealand at that time an overseas sit-com such as *Alf* could be expected to yield the NZBC between $45,000 and $50,000 for an outlay of around $1100 per episode (Lealand 1988). These figures suggest that the commercials are often constructed with more care and at more cost per minute than the programmes which surround them (Arlen 1980).

Their local significance is further revealed by the clear and present tendency to expand the amount of television time given over to advertising. Sundays are no longer exempt. As recently as the late 1980s the permitted daily average that was sanctioned by TVNZ's rules was (an internationally high) nine minutes per hour of advertising, with a maximum of twenty minutes in any two hours. Since then it has edged upwards by a third as much again. Read traditionally, however, as in the correspondence columns of the *Listener*, the programmes are still seen as primary and the commercials are merely their irritating adjuncts—they should be kept in their place. The general tone of such letters is thus one of exasperation at the invasion of private pleasures, of anger at the intrusion of someone else's brats, uninvited guests who have strayed into the bedroom of our desires. But when broadcasting revenue is overwhelmingly derived from advertising, property displaces propriety. Programmes are open house and viewers are open season. From being an instrument of broadcasting strategy, advertising has become its determining environment. The prime function of the programmes has become the delivery of audiences to advertisers; the centre of gravity has shifted towards the commercials themselves. From such a perspective the commercials are not interruptions: they are the foundation of the entire process; a definitive expression of the official culture of capitalism and the basis on which

New Zealand broadcasting systems seek to reproduce themselves. It is therefore hardly surprising that 'spot the ideology' in commercials has become an acceptable alternative to Trivial Pursuit as a parlour game for the academic left, or that 'spot the commercial' has become a scholarly obligation for observers of children's street and schoolyard games.

Coming up next, an item on Noises in the Head. But first, an endorsement of our product/programme by someone you may know and trust ∴ . .

• • •

Roland Barthes on Interrupting the Text: or Br(e)aking (for) Commercials:

> There should pass through the essay's discourse from time to time, a sensual object (as in *Werther*, where suddenly there appears a dish of green peas cooked in butter and a peeled orange separated into sections). A double advantage: sumptuous appearance of a materiality and a distortion, a sudden gap wedged into the intellectual murmur . . .
>
> Is there not a kind of voluptuous pleasure in inserting, like a perfumed dream, into a sociological analysis, 'wild cherries, cinnamon, vanilla, and sherry, Canadian tea, lavender, bananas?' . . . or again, to introduce into a sociological journal 'brocade trousers, capes and the long white nightshirts' worn by hippies? Once you let a 'bluish circle of smoke' into critical discourse, you can find the courage, quite simply . . . *to copy it over*. (Barthes 1977, p.135, italics in original)

• • •

For Barthes, this process is an exemplar of *jouissance* and a model for liberation from the confines of orthodox literary and critical practice. Yet for Williams a strikingly analogous sequence in a different medium is seen as the expression of a disturbing orthodoxy, the impetus for his claim that the distinctiveness of television is to be found in the highly organised matter-of-factness of such discontinuities. Such discrepant responses can, of course, be contained by pointing to the contrast between the respective discursive spaces occupied by Williams's Anglo-Saxon cultural Marxism and Barthes's Gallic post-structuralism—as well as the differences between watching television and writing literary essays. But despite the snare lines laid around these passages by such theoretical machinery, my sense of being strongly drawn to both of them is undiminished. Such snare lines are both invaluable guides for explorers and potential traps for the unwary. The sound of those traps closing shut, of clamps being placed on the imagination, may displace, but it does not still, the rustle of these texts. Such traces not only signify an origin that is simply elsewhere, but an elsewhere that, in its turn, is a signifier for signs of life. What is pointed to is not the blissful clarity of myth but the whispered residue of a creative presence. It is perfectly captured (how else to phrase it?) by Barthes's observation that 'Writing is that *play* by which I turn around as well as I can in a narrow space' (Barthes 1977, p.137, italics in original).

The precondition of the conversation between Williams and Barthes that takes place in my—and now your—head is a shared aversion to closure and a common concern to render tacit structures visible. In each case they offer us texts about texts. In each case they write (speak) as a reader and in each case they invite another kind of reading. But whereas Williams is striving to document the textual consequences of centralised production in a culture industry, Barthes writes reflexively as, and about, an individual artisan investigating the limits of, and the limits on, his craft. Put another way, Williams's aim is to enable the reader the better to *see* (through the working of his text), whereas the Barthesian effect is to enable the reader the better to *see through* the working of his text. This echoes a distinction which Barthes (1975) made elsewhere (where else?) between 'readerly' (i.e. familiar, reassuring, reinforcing) and 'writerly' (i.e. unsettling, disturbing, polyphonic) texts. On behalf of the reader Barthes the writer prioritises writerly texts. For insofar as they make the reader more conscious of her own activity, such works facilitate her movement from passive consumer to active producer of the text. I want to briefly indicate how reading the writerly Barthes alongside Williams's readerly text can be conducive to such an effect. The point being made is, of course, that Williams's readerly text has a flow of its own, which can be slowed down or interrupted by (the imaginary conversation with) Barthes.

What Williams calls 'the single irresponsible flow of images and feelings' seems an apposite metonym for a medium and a culture that is overwhelmingly based upon the continued generation of wants, but is increasingly unable or unwilling to organise them into an evaluative hierarchy. It was just such a combination which had brought the culture industry theorists Adorno and Horkheimer (1979) to a condition of terminal despair—and their famous analysis predates television. Although

Williams was concerned to remain not just exempt from, but actively opposed to, the Frankfurt School authors' gloomy (and flawed) conception of a mass culture and a mass audience, both the residue of their prognosis and the ghost of Leavis are at work in his own account. They are there, for example, in the privileging of narrative and in the associated dependence upon an over-literary conception of the reading process. What is posited is a pattern of attention through which the viewer attends single-mindedly and continuously to whatever is being screened. Hence the Miami sequence becomes 'a very difficult experience to interpret'. Yet at the same time the blending together of 'images and feelings' collapses the reader's response into that authorised by the cultural form of the medium. The work *of* the reader is seen as given by how flow works *on* the reader. But 'flow' can be read not just as the commercially induced drive to reconcile disparate narratives with television's own cultural conventions, but also as the industry's overdetermined attempt to hold the reader/viewer when the normal condition of viewing is one of selective (in)attention. That is to say, viewers themselves routinely introduce their own interruptions into the television text (cf. for example, Ellis 1982; Morley 1986).

• • •

We will return to the reader shortly. Please stay tuned for this important message from the star of our show . . .

> Each society classifies objects in its own way, and this way constitutes the very intelligibility it grants itself . . .
> We classify products according to a rational typology: fruits here, drinks there, etc: this is a lazy verbal classification . . . Lévi-Strauss shows that other groupings can be made: a certain 'logic of perception' will lead to grouping wild cherries, cinnamon, vanilla and sherry here, and there Labrador tea, lavender, bananas . . .
> His observations are entirely corroborated by a semantic analysis of the texts of Fashion: despite appearances (Fashion appears to wield a great profusion of colours) contemporary Fashion knows only two main signifying groups of colours (they are, of course, in opposition): the 'marked' colours (*high-coloured*) and the 'neutral' colours; carried in a sense by this opposition, intelligibility can nicely divide one and the same colour: there are brilliant blacks and dull blacks, and it is this very opposition which signifies, not the opposition, for example, of black and white. (Barthes 1988, pp.166–7)

Thanks Roland, not only for providing us with food for thought but also for bringing a little colour into our lives—even if it is all black . . .

• • •

The suggestion of an opposition between two kinds of black is a way into the Steinlager All Black commercials which were screened in the build-up to the Rugby World Cup final in 1987. In order to provide support for this argument it is important to note that those commercials also reflected the fact that in 1986 and early 1987 Steinlager had been a sponsor, and beneficiary, of the KZ7 America's Cup challenge that was briefly considered in Chapter Two. We saw how this was an event that was made for, and by, corporate interests. But we also saw how by comparison with rugby, yachting was a sport which could be presented as permeated by new high-tech indicators of masculine power, as more attractive to women, as more explicitly subordinate to commercial considerations, and in which international sporting competition and economic interests could be seen to work in tandem. By contrast, rugby's traditional claim to be the custodian of New Zealand's national pride had been severely damaged by the 1981 tour, the abandoned 1985 tour of South Africa and the rebel tour by the Cavaliers (cf. Fougere 1989).

That contrast was effectively dramatised by an evening's viewing on 7 October 1986. Between 8 and 9 pm, TV2 featured *The New Zealand Challenge*, a programme on the background and build-up to KZ7's bid for the America's Cup. It made much play of the parallels between being in charge of a business office and in charge of a twelve-metre yacht. What was effectively signalled was a conception of masculinity congruent with corporate structures, computer technology and sporting activity. It was preceded by *University Challenge* at 7.30 and followed by *Cagney and Lacey* at 9.00. In what might have seemed a wry commentary on emerging social trends in New Zealand it thus found itself sandwiched between popular images of the young, ambitious, educated middle class and popular images of the new woman. Over on TV1 the 9 pm documentary was Sue Kedgley's presentation of *A Little Bit Tough—The Rise and Fall of the Rugby Man* (sitting uneasily, if no less ironically, between *Home to Roost* at 8.30 and *The Professionals* at 10.00).

A feminist's critique of rugby during prime time? Clearly some kind of cultural barrier had been breached. It provided an echo, within the most popular medium, of a rhetorical question which Helen White (1985, p.492) had posed in *Landfall*. In her review of the 1985 revival of *Foreskin's Lament*, she had asked, 'Who would have thought that five years would have turned this one into a period piece?' In 1980/81, the force of Greg McGee's play had at once depended upon and expressed the way 'rugby' and 'nation' could be seen as interchangeable terms. By the mid-1980s it was possible, but simply no longer plausible, to see them as coextensive. By 1986 the kind of difficulties involved in updating *Foreskin's Lament* seemed to be at one with the difficulties which faced rugby as a game. Neither could now credibly claim to carry the full weight of representing the cultural identity of a society undergoing change.

Just a few years later, however, and despite its basic script remaining largely unaltered, rugby is certainly no period piece. What has been changed is its advance publicity (towards new corporate sponsors), its stage management (towards television), its direction (towards commercialism) and its cast of players (towards professionalism). And it played before packed houses at a major drama festival in 1987 (the World Cup). It has, as it were, been corporatised, and the resulting change in its image might be said to have been prefigured by *The New Zealand Challenge* programme which TV2 screened just before the Kedgley documentary on TV1. As we saw in Chapter Two, Fougere's argument was that the origins of rugby's claim to represent the nation had rested upon the way the game had grown from the bottom up. By contrast, the public conception of twelve-metre yacht racing as a sport had been constructed from the top down, a product of combining the ingenuity and interests of television technologies and corporate actors. Clearly there were lessons to be drawn. Could the enormous popular appeal of KZ7, and the success story it represented for Steinlager as a major sponsor, be generalised to other sports and other contexts? Could rugby be rescued from the doldrums by the World Cup competition? Could a premium beer and a premiere team be made to make the perfect match? Could the interests of the corporate system and those of rugby be made to meet? Did Black have a future?

It was just such an endeavour to change the sport's image, and through it the attempt to respond to the social order in which it is located, which was given expression in the 1987 Steinlager All Black commercials made for Steinlager by the Mackay King agency. These involved the presentation of a highly stylised microcosm of an international game—what

Black/marketing: Steinlager's 1987 All Black commercial.

follows focuses on a sixty-second version designed to represent an All Black victory over Australia. But first, this testimonial from a distinguished European *auteur* . . .

● ● ●

After watching some clips of British television commercials, the Italian film director Federico Fellini was reported to have said, 'How can these people produce such little masterpieces lasting one minute?'(Watson & Hill 1984, p.97) (He subsequently went on to make one of his own for Martini.)

And now, back to our commercial . . .

• • •

The opening shot is of an Australian aboriginal, purportedly in a desert
location and engaged in a traditional dance (we hear a didgeridoo). It is
shot against the dramatic background of a sky that is bright red and
portrayed through the use of time lapse photography. This cuts to a shot
of four All Blacks performing the haka against a black background, and
then cuts back to the Australian location, this time to portray a jackaroo,
complete with full outback gear and saddle (there are echoes here of the
Marlboro Man, albeit one who signifies some anxiety and self doubt
about what is to come). He is shown in both middle distance and close

up. This is followed by rapid cutting between close-up images of limb movements in the haka, shots of the aboriginal figure, and the four All Blacks. This leads into the extremely stylised representation of the game itself, complete with images of successful All Black tackling, line-out possession, running and try scoring, shot mostly in close up and always in slow motion. The action is tightly synchronised to the sound of John Lennon's 'Stand By Me' (which was also the title of a 'bonding' movie about teenage boys that had recently played in local cinemas). The background is black throughout, the sequences are dramatically backlit and the game is portrayed as if in a continuous downpour. The final try is, however, scored against the open background of a lightening sky, displays a real set of posts and is shown through a middle-distance shot. The commercial comes to a close with the Australian player signifying the end of the game, and his (team's) defeat, through the ritual exchange of jerseys. The final shot shows the Australian and an All Black turning together to walk off towards the sunrise; the frame is frozen, and a Steinlager label is superimposed across their shorts.

The commercial encodes a preferred reading. For example, the contrast between dry (Australia) and wet (New Zealand) is one way of invoking the idea of beer at a time when television's advertising rules debarred the showing of the product itself. And whereas Australia is signified by both Aboriginal and European, they are shown separately and as the incumbents of contrasting cultures. Against this, the All Blacks are shown to be both Maori and Pakeha, both team members and individuals (the commercial tends to focus on Michael Jones and Sean Fitzpatrick), united in and by the haka. The delicate skip of the Aboriginal and the anxious face of the jackaroo (signifying womanly action and wimpish thoughts?) are counterposed against the confident body movements of the haka—the rain and lighting allowing the muscularity of the latter to be shot in high definition. We saw in Chapter Four that there are several entertaining precedents for this use of Australia(ns) in New Zealand television commercials both as a way of defining what is local and controlling that definition. The distinctiveness of the Steinlager commercial is therefore not to be found in its use of 'Australia' (or 'Wales' for that matter) but in its overall *look*.

Let me try and develop this. What is most striking about the iconography of the commercial is the way it calls attention to its own artificiality. It is frequently back lit, deploys cropped and composed images of the male body and strives for an absence of visual clutter. Camera move- ment is kept to a minimum, effects are achieved through the precisely synchronised cutting and the change of lenses. What is at work here is the kind of disposition in which aesthetic appeal is seen as residing in the 'mode of representation' rather than being a 'property of the subject'. It is a disposition which gives priority to *the way* something is shown rather than *what* is being shown. In Bourdieu's account (1984) such differences in taste are seen as closely linked to differences in educational level and can serve as a proxy for social class differences. Let us call them Type 1 and Type 2 tastes respectively. An agency responsible for an up-market beer seeking to broaden its base might be expected to employ distinc- tively Type 1 means to show the kind of subject popular amongst those with Type 2 preferences. Type 1 audiences might be expected to respond to the form of the commercial, Type 2 to its subject matter—and the social division between these discrepant readings is blurred by a text which allows for both.

Put another way, if we make use of Barthes's observation that it is the distinction between two kinds of black which signifies, then it is clear that this commercial is constructed *across* that difference. From black as utilitarian to black as glamorous, from matter-of-fact black to designer black, from black as ordinary to black as exclusive, from black as invisible to black as visible, from black as simply given to black as consciously made, from Type 2 black to Type 1 black. Black, that is, as the aesthetic expression of an expanding corporate system, with 'the creeping multi- plicity of black objects as part of the creeping hegemony of the young middle class' (Rambali 1985, p.48).

Thus far I have sought to show that this commercial both expresses, and endeavours to control for ethnic and class divisions amongst its audience. It does so by putting into circulation a set of meanings that can be shared across (or failing that, will at least admit of being selectively read from) discrepant social locations. This helps to account for some- thing of its look. What has so far been neglected, however, and what needs to be registered is that there is about this ad a fullness, an over-the- top quality. It is as if Colin Meads were to script Mills and Boon, having just seen Coppola's *Apocalypse Now* and Fassbinder's *Querelle*. In other words, it is Camp—and the best-known guide to this domain is New York's Susan Sontag:

As a taste in persons, Camp responds particularly to the markedly attenuated and to the strongly exaggerated. The androgyne is certainly one of the great images of Camp sensibility. Here Camp taste draws on a mostly unacknowledged truth of taste: the most refined form of sexual attractiveness (as well as the most refined form of sexual pleasure) consists of going against the grain of one's sex. What is most beautiful in virile men is something feminine; what is most beautiful in feminine women is something masculine . . .

Camp sees everything in quotation marks. It's not a lamp but a 'lamp' not a woman but a 'woman' . . .

Thus the Camp sensibility is one that is alive to a double sense in which some things can be taken. But this is not the familiar split-level construction of a literal meaning, on the one hand, and a symbolic meaning on the other. It is the difference rather between the thing as meaning something, anything, and the thing as pure artifice . . . (Sontag 1966, pp.279–81)

My understanding is that the agency's remit was to present the All Blacks in a way that would appeal to women. (This is viewed with incredulity by most of the women I know, but the agency's correspondence file tells a different story. It also suggests that the choice of 'Stand By Me' as the musical backing was designed to invoke not just male bonding but female support.) I am interested in the agency's intention only insofar as it helps to explain such images as the close-up of Sean Fitzpatrick's narcissistic gaze into the camera lens, or the cutting up of men's bodies (thighs, waist-to-knee shots) in ways that have been made familiar by the portrayal of women in advertising. The assumptions of the male gaze (Mulvey 1975; but cf. Gamman & Marshment 1988) are applied by men to men but on behalf of women. The presumption of a female viewer thus leads to the production of a male version of what it is like to read like a (heterosexual) woman. The resulting images are charged with sexual ambiguity. More particularly, they problematise the position of the heterosexual male viewer. He is confronted with Fitzpatrick's come hither look or Michael Jones flashing thighs, shot in that lyrical slow motion that is characteristic of the portrayal of both sport replays and lovemaking. Whatever the intention, this commercial is clearly available for a distinctively gay reading.

Sontag notes, but does not really develop the point, that there are strong affinities between camp sensibility and a gay aesthetic. Irrespective of sexual orientation, however, it would seem that creative work in advertising is very conducive to the development of a such a sensibility—

since it is a particularly useful strategy for distancing the self, amongst those obliged to work on, or with, material that does not inspire trust.

Inasmuch as camp is a way of dealing with cultural dominance, its local significance extends beyond gays and advertising professionals. A specifically 'antipodean camp', in the form of sardonic distancing and stylised subversion, is to found in cultural practices as discrete as some parts of Ian Wedde's poetry, the children's television programme *Terry and the Gunrunners*, TV3's *Nightline*, Count Robula and (intermittently) the public persona of David Lange (cf. Perry 1990, pp. 91-92). When so much of our conceptual baggage and cultural equipment is imported/imposed, a receptivity to the exposure of (some aspects of) culture as artifice is itself a local cultural characteristic. This trait has its bleaker, mean-spirited side and there are plenty of blind spots, notably a cripplingly sentimental cultural nationalism in everything from best-selling management textbooks to the design of export logos. But with a few commendable exceptions (e.g. Buchanan 1984; Lealand 1988; Openshaw & Shuker 1988) what has been neglected is the hard-(l)earned capacity of many New Zealanders to make something of their lives through the production of local readings, inflections and uses of derivative cultural material. Where such material comes from has been emphasised, what people *do* with it has been overlooked. I want simply to note that local circumstances may sometimes be conducive to a selective and creative reading and innovative use of apparently unpromising texts—and that antipodean camp is supportive of such usages.

To give three brief examples. The first is how, at the age of thirteen, our elder daughter and her friends devised a common tactic for disarming (*sic*) the unwanted (adolescent) male gaze by making use of a widely shared aspect of the contemporary adolescent's viewing habits. In a parody of a parody they imitated, in tone of voice, in gesture and in bodily deportment the way Con the Fruiterer says 'looking, looking' in the Australian television series *The Comedy Company*.

The second is from Brisbane at the time of the Bjelke Petersen bid to become prime minister (I did say antipodean camp!). Bumper stickers began to appear in the green and white colours of the Country Party proclaiming 'Joh for PM'. An enterprising Queenslander promptly produced a much better selling version, identical except that it read 'ALF for PM', at a time when the American sit-com was particularly popular in the state. And a yet more enterprising ploy was to amend the originals so that they read 'Joh for PMT'. (There are echoes here of that time in New Zealand politics when the most effective opposition to Muldoon was being provided by cartoonist Tom Scott.)

The third is a short film by the Auckland director Peter Wells called *Give 'Em a Taste of Kiwi*. It makes use of some of the images from the Steinlager and other beer and rugby commercials, intercut with explicit shots of gay sex (the Kiwi Taste is fellatio) and a soundtrack in which orgasmic grunts form a counterpoint to the 'Give 'Em a Taste of Kiwi' refrain. At the screening which I saw (at the *Now See Hear!* symposium in Wellington) Wells introduced it with a particularly forthright and perceptive critique of homophobia.

The point about these three instances of cultural work is that although they require relatively modest or no resources, they make use of centrally produced and widely known imagery and meanings. They are not Fellini's 'little masterpieces' but something more important, namely, little victories. They are signs of resistance which use the signs of control. They serve as advertisements for our better selves, interruptions of the texts of power.

And now for something completely different . . .

●   ●   ●

There is a Samuel Beckett play called *Breath*. It is set on an empty stage. The lights go up. There is the sound of a single breath. The lights go down.

The play can be read as the end of life—or the beginning. Or the time between. The entire process is around thirty seconds long.[2]

---

1 Compare, for example, Margaret Rose's (1978) structuralist account of parody and its limits in the young Marx and Engels with that classic 'work of the break', Rosa and Charley Parkin's 'Peter Rabbit and the Grundrisse' (1974).

2 Since this was first published (in 1990) a commercial sponsored by the Ministry of Transport has appeared on our screens (in March 1993). Its subject is the introduction of random stopping for breathalyser tests; its (minimalist) content consists of visual images of the words 'Anytime, Anywhere, Anyone' fading in and out to the sound of a single breath. The formal precedent may have been provided by similar low-budget commercials for Telecom, but one wonders what Beckett would have made of it— especially when it punctuates the British serial *Waiting for God*!

SIX

Am I Rite? Or am I Write? Or am I Right?

A New Zealand Reading of *The Singing Detective*

Textual meanings exhibit an incorrigible instability, and the meaning of the term 'text' is resolutely indeterminate. Chapter Five can be read as wavering between a celebratory recognition of these points and a determined effort to control (for) them. More generally, a premiss of this book is that family photographs and abstract paintings, old movies and new clothes, traditional academic papers and contemporary popular music videos, can all be read as texts. This should be a commonplace. Yet the local implications of such a platitude have barely been explored. The dominant forms of textual interpretation and cultural analysis in this country continue to express those notoriously over-literary emphases which have long been characteristic of the Anglo-American intelligentsia. The *Listener*'s attitude towards television was for many years symptomatic of this tendency. Until the 1990s (and the arrival of Diana Wichtel) it persisted in employing television critics who did not even *like* the medium (Camille Guy was a creditable exception, a commendably open and responsive reviewer during her brief sojourn).

This might, of course, be interpreted as the unanticipated consequence of a wayward personnel policy, or perhaps as evidence of one magazine's struggle to distance itself from that material base on which its claim to cultural centrality effectively rested. To see it as signalling a problem of criticism involves a shift of focus—away from one of the (once) favoured institutions of the New Zealand intelligentsia, and towards their own preferred subject matter and methods of working. From this perspective the *Listener*'s stratagem is symptomatic of a wider failure of critical practice; a pattern in which the dominant tendency is a malign neglect of television, and in which prescribing the attitude to be taken towards a given programme becomes a substitute for trying to understand how such texts achieve their effects. The procedural conventions of such a narrowly conceived approach can engage neither with television as a medium nor with the sheer diversity of its content.

Critics elsewhere have gravitated towards an emphasis on one or the other of these features, with their preference shaped according to whether they have been impressed by television's uniformity or by its variety. Two of the best-known, but contrasting, stances were those adopted by Marshall McLuhan in the 1960s and by Clive James in the 1970s. McLuhan (1964, p.32) fleshed out his well-known claim that the medium is the message by describing content as 'the juicy piece of meat carried by a burglar to distract the watchdog of the mind'. Food for thought, no doubt. In his column for Britain's *Observer* Clive James was no less sardonic (he once described an Ingmar Bergman teleplay as 'muesli without milk'). He saw in the content of television a rich feast of critical possibilities, a cultural smorgasbord which perfectly catered to his overdeveloped sense of wit. The result is a marvellous source of after-dinner one-liners. James has a gift for puncturing cultural pretensions, a talent for quipping against the pricks. If read against the high seriousness of his essays on Russian literature (cf. James 1982), however, James's response to television seems glib and formulaic, and the medium's specificities seem neglected. When, for example, the theatre critic Kenneth Tynan suggested to him that television criticism was impossible because it required you to 'know everything',[1] James was initially nonplussed. It was rather like inviting a longtime street fighter to think like a referee. His belated but characteristic response was to declare himself heartened by a recognition that even though he couldn't claim omniscience, nor could anyone else.

The episode is instructive. When George Bernard Shaw observed of a particularly disastrous theatrical first night that, 'This play had everything, but is everything enough?', he was being no less pertinent than Tynan and no less witty than James. What Shaw's remark relies upon is a readership attuned to the indispensable role of theatrical convention. In like fashion it is the conventions of television which provide a way into a critical understanding of the medium. What Tynan overlooks is the distinction between the language *of* television and the language *on* television (Silverstone 1981, p.38). It is precisely this difference between the (restricted) forms of discourse that are distinctive to television and those which are characteristic of the profusion of voices, subjects and themes that it appropriates, which both McLuhan and James are inclined to neglect. They also neglect the ways in which the component features of this bewildering plurality interact both with each other and with the expectations of the audience. Their respective emphases (on the global properties of the medium and on the details of a given programme) mean that their engagement with such considerations is, at best, oblique. What is missing is a recognition that the structure of television discourse is conditioned, but not determined, by the technology of production, and that it is expressed through signifiers whose promiscuity it regulates but does not prescribe.

It is this determination at the level of discourse which accounts for television's very intelligibility—the fact that it can be read by so many— and this is both a measure of its cultural achievement and the basis of a critical approach. Far from being impossible, television criticism is splendidly democratic. Not only do most of us do it, but most of us *can* do it. Where Tynan views this in terms of the limits it places on the idea of the professional critic and the privileged interpretation, the opportunity it offers is for a realignment of critical practice, in which the question 'how does it work?' assumes priority over the puzzle of 'what does it mean?' This intrinsically sociological stance depends upon probing the way in which the cultural habits of both audience and producers intersect so as to produce a possible meaning. The subject of such a criticism is the forms of tacit knowledge on which this cultural interaction depends, and its purpose is to subvert television's 'blissful clarity' (cf. Barthes 1973, p.143) to recover a sense of its strangeness.

Which edges us a little nearer to *The Singing Detective*. Like the exchange between Tynan and James, the series was produced in Britain (with Australian support). Like most of our television, it was neither made by, nor made for, New Zealanders. The most appropriate critical path for us, therefore, is that line which charts the text's conditions of legibility. We need to recover not just its encoded (or preferred) meaning, but to probe into the cultural and material circumstances which made the series possible; to consider what made it possible for us to read it and to try and identify the audience for which it selects and to whom it might speak.

The series was first screened in Britain in November and December

1986 and in New Zealand a year later. It might well have been termed 'the BBC's Christmas present to itself', had not *Edge of Darkness* previously attracted such an epithet (Penman 1986, p.76). In other words, it was a series in which a greater measure of discretion appears to have been granted to the production team as a whole, and to the writer in particular, than is usually the case. Moreover this occurred within a broadcasting organisation in which the claim (if not the fact) of autonomy is itself given more forceful institutional expression than is usually the case. Both the critical response to the series and the BBC's own profile of writer Dennis Potter,[2] suggested that here was something special. If the notion of '*auteur*' status is capable of migrating to television from its origins in the study of film,[3] then it seemed that Potter could plausibly lay claim to such a title. The series itself could conceivably have been made for Britain's Channel Four (an organisation whose existence is itself predicated upon the prior presence of the BBC). It could never have been made for the American networks.

It does, however—and however obliquely—exhibit the signs of the networks' presence. My suggestion is that the discourse of contemporary British television can only be understood (whether by the British, or by ourselves) in relation to its US counterpart. Probing the properties of American television is thus a preamble to isolating what is distinctive about the British.

First, and most obviously, the US networks are simply too intent on reconciling audience targets with corporate control to relinquish very much of the latter to a production team, let alone to a writer. It is, however, a misleading and sentimental conceit to read this in terms of a distinction between the BBC's principled support of culture and the American networks' venal commercialism. Nor is it just the idea of difference which makes a difference. All television discourse is permeated by both market pressures and hierarchical controls (cf. Farnsworth 1992). What is problematic is the way these factors articulate so as to produce variations in programming and in typical modes of inflection. That process resists being reduced to a contrast between Art and Commerce. That redundant distinction simply cannot provide the leverage to explain such minor miracles as the early *Hill Street Blues*, a cop show whose pleasures I hinted at in Chapter Three. Here was a network series distinguished by open and complex multiple plotting (derived from the soaps), characterisation of some depth, and a knowing and affectionate reworking of *film noir* conventions. The Art/Commerce contrast also precludes any recognition, or engagement with, the visual accomplishments (derived from rock videos and commercials) of so resolutely non-literary and politically retrograde a series as *Miami Vice.*

The terrain between post-liberal blues (Gitlin 1983, p.308) and postmodernist vice (Fiske 1987, p.118) is the location for a strategic skirmish, part of the contested ground in a wider struggle to define the agenda for a popular culture which may be American in origin but is global in its reach. The success of *Miami Vice* signals just how far the terms of that engagement are now weighted towards the visual, rather than the literary.

What is at stake are notions of cultural centrality. Thus *LA Law*, as its title suggests, can be seen as a response to *Miami Vice*. It is a series produced by the team responsible for *Hill Street Blues* and although it embodies some of *Hill Street*'s virtues, it altogether lacks the visual texture of that earlier series. *Hill Street* was conditioned by the injunction to 'make it look messy'. Hence the graininess, the shadowy, imperfectly lit scenes, the occasional use of hand-held cameras, the frequent dislocation of privileged narratives by the movement of other actors within the frame, the emphasis on sombre-toned blues, greys and browns. In *LA Law* the only messiness is interpersonal and it has no visual correlate. Yet it is possible to envisage how the settings and the way they are shot, could, as in both *Hill Street* and *Miami Vice*, be employed to consciously mirror or disrupt the dominant narrative. Thus although *LA Law* makes use of sight gags, it seems visually retrograde by comparison. Not because it has too many suits and too many suites, but because of how they are shown. The ingenuity with which the designs of its protagonists are explored is not matched by a comparable visual exploration of corporate design.

Nonetheless *LA Law*, like *Hill Street* and *Miami Vice*, is indebted, and gives textual expression, to the organisational continuities between network television and Hollywood cinema. And it was, of course, Hollywood in its heyday which prefigured the world market in images, developed the authoritative narrative models, and orchestrated appropriate conceptions of visual literacy. Dominant cinema has metamorphosed into dominant television and thus defines the field on which the BBC is obliged to play.

As Dick Hebdige (1982) has documented, the hostility of Britain's opinion-makers and cultural custodians to this 'Americanisation' of popular culture goes back at least as far as the 1930s. The terms in which such fears are couched have remained remarkably constant for more than fifty years. An indigenous and authentic Britishness (or more often English-ness) is set against the corrupt and corrupting influences which American culture purportedly embodies. It's a pattern of response which links the writings of a misanthropic high Tory like Evelyn Waugh to George Orwell's 1940s essays on popular culture, to Richard Hoggart's *The Uses of Literacy* in 1957 and to Martin Esslin's *The Age of Television* in 1983.[4] Its impact in and on the BBC has been most evident in quality English drama (or q.e.d. in Alex Calder's felicitous acronym [1987]), but its influence has been pervasive.

Such sentiments have proved remarkably resilient in the face of their continual subversion by popular taste. They are, however, incorporated in a body of thought which, like Marlow's body at the beginning of *The Singing Detective*, is now in crisis. When being British means watching *Dallas*, it also means that a literary conception of culture is faced with a crisis of representation, and a nationalist conception of culture is faced with a crisis of jurisdiction. One response to the presence of so many cultural space invaders is imperiously to bemoan cultural imperialism from the foxholes scattered throughout publishing, higher education and the quality press. Thus Mike Poole's survey of the backgrounds of British television reviewers (1984) shows how their criticism, like ours, reads like a conspiracy of the literary against the laity. By contrast, those British intellectuals who choose to work in television are confronted on a day-to-day basis with the incentive to work the crisis through. And that is precisely what *The Singing Detective* attempts to do.

Like Marlow's own long, slow process of deterioration, the onset of present difficulties can be traced back to, and was triggered by, indisput-able evidence of betrayal and an end to innocence. With the arrival of commercial television in the mid-1950s the BBC, like Marlow's father, was cuckolded. Furthermore the British public, like Marlow's mother, proved to be willing participants in their own seduction. Both they and she decamped. Thus Jane Root notes that by September 1957 British commercial television had gained 79 per cent of the audience. She goes on to cite Peter Black's observation that 'The audience's goodwill towards the monopoly turned out to be an illusion. Once they had a choice, the working class left the BBC at a pace which suggested ill will was more deeply entrenched than good' (Root 1986, p.61). Both the British public and Marlow's mother had been subject to the austere constraints and the dead weight of an authority which (whether in the form of in-laws or control of broadcasting) had sought to regulate their domestic activities. Each of these authorities had sought to legitimate their control in the name of a common culture and common decency. But each expressed a conception of the past, rather than their subjects' own sense of the present or their image of the future. Neither the British public nor Marlow's mother wanted any part of it. Their anthem was American—'Don't Fence Me In'. Their actual seducer had less to offer, of course, but was nonetheless just sharp enough, possessed just enough of the requisite amount of gloss, to be a vehicle for their suppressed desires and their impulse to escape.

Although in each case the entire process of seduction was observed, it was only imperfectly understood at the time, whether by Marlow or by the British cultural establishment. Its implications were, however, clearly disturbing. In each case there was a need to believe that the prevailing conception of identity (whether personal or national) was still intact, that nothing had really changed. In each case this depended upon a lie at the centre; and upon allocating blame for the public presence of one's own shit to someone else. There it lay in the schoolroom of the nation, disrupting the authorised lessons. It could not be ignored. Authority, whether in the shape of a patriotic schoolmistress, or cultural apologists for BBC 'standards', was receptive to the idea that it was the least intelligent who were at fault (in the accents of such a 'hit and miss' authority, 'mess' could even sound like 'mass'). The denied and dirty little secret, however, was that the threat to identity came not from without, but from within. Such a secret could only be spoken obliquely, refracted through fictions, manifested in signs of disturbance, transformed into a foreign body (whether by Marlow or by the British cultural establishment).

Thus for the adult Marlow, his mother's villainous suitor subsequently appears in two different guises. In his detective story he is the (upper class) agent of a foreign power, a betrayer of secrets; in his interpretation of the present he is a go-between for Hollywood interests, the seducer and betrayer of Marlow's ex-wife. Acts of personal betrayal are thus fused with the repudiation of Britishness, in which villainy consists of an embracing of alien elements, a denial of community membership. But the childhood Marlow offers a much more ambiguous interpretation of the community response to the original seduction, the event from which these later fictions derive. Like his perception of family and of self, his perception of community is split. It is therefore seen by him—and shown to us—as at once comforting and threatening. For example, he and we see the village pub as the site of communal sentiment (orchestrated by his father), as a location for (his mother's) uneasy duplicity and as a place of collective menace.

For the adult Marlow striving to come to terms with the debilitating effects of this split, story-telling is a psychic necessity: part therapy, part evasion. The matrix from which a solution to crisis can be constructed is that psychic and cultural territory which lies between what he is and what his hero is, between his story and his detective('s) story. Marlow was, of course, the name of an earlier psychological investigator and cultural explorer, the narrator of Joseph Conrad's *Heart of Darkness* (the BBC having explored its edge the year before). Like Conrad's protagonist, Marlow as hospital patient embarks upon a journey into his own past. But in any such exploration a guide recruited from the ranks of literary high culture is in danger of being either too quixotic or of travelling in only the narrowest of channels (however deep they may be). His indispensable aide-memoire and Sancho Panza is therefore Marlow as singing detective, and this Marlow has a trans-atlantic namesake (albeit with an 'e') in the form of the private-eye hero of Raymond Chandler's novels. Chandler's work occupied a profoundly ambiguous position in relation to the contrast between being British and being American. His novels were set in Los Angeles and steeped in the US vernacular, but his detective was imbued with moral principles that critics variously interpreted as commendable English integrity, as hard-boiled decency, or as a somewhat improbable public-school propriety. Marlow's singing detective signals such cultural ambiguity in a much more conscious fashion. His musical tastes (which, given the 1940s setting, predate television) are both popular and resolutely British (whereas Marlow's mother was shown as preferring Bing Crosby and the Andrews Sisters). But his laconic patterns of speech nod towards Hollywood, and although his accent is hardly mid-Atlantic it is manifestly off-shore. *The Singing Detective* therefore incorporates a recognition that 'Americanisation' was an identifiable aspect of British popular culture by the 1940s. George Orwell was amongst those who had deeply objected to this development and in 'Raffles to Miss Blandish' he identified the crime story as symptomatic of what had changed. But as Orwell (1957) himself had pointed out, the English author of the 'Americanised' book which offended him (*No Orchids for Miss Blandish*) had never been to America.

What is implicit in the cultural argument of *The Singing Detective* is that Orwell had chosen the wrong writer, focused on the wrong book and drawn the wrong conclusions. Chandler may have lived in America, but he was an English-educated anglophile whose hardback sales and literary standing were much better in Britain than in the United States (cf. Gardiner & Walker 1962, pp.149, 169, 173). Above all, he had provided a critically important solution to the problem of how to reconcile a popular cultural form with the aesthetic standards of high culture. That is a preoccupation which the *The Singing Detective* knowingly replicates. For example, the death of the 1940s villain in the final episode of the series is unexplained, but we learn that a note beside the body reads, 'Who cares who killed Roger Ackroyd?' *The Murder of Roger Ackroyd* is an Agatha Christie story in which the narrator is the murderer, but the reference is to the title of an Edmund Wilson essay. That essay singled out Chandler for positive comment, and together with some comments by W. H. Auden, was important in helping to bring his work to the attention of high-culture critics.

Chandler's solution to these Anglo/American and high culture/popular culture dilemmas was a literary one. But as the film critic Dilys Powell noted in her review of *Double Indemnity* (for which Chandler and Billy Wilder had written the screenplay), 'Chandler's writing at its best is sharply visual, getting its effects by observed detail' (cited in Macshane 1976, p.108).[5] What Chandler's books depend upon is a way of writing in which the imagery is rather more memorable than the convolutions of the plot. For example, Phillip French (1977, p.71) notes that when Howard Hawks was directing *The Big Sleep*, he and his screenwriters asked Chandler who had killed General Sternwood's chauffeur. They gave up worrying about it on discovering that not even he could remember. One consequence of Chandler's cinematic literary style is that his cultural significance and impact has been rather different in Britain from in the United States. That first screenplay secured his reputation in Hollywood, and his work prefigured that developed visual sensibility which is characteristic of contemporary American television and popular films.

I have briefly indicated the ways in which *Hill Street Blues* and *Miami*

Vice give expression to this and suggested something of its implications for the BBC. It also helps to explain the huge popular success and critical disdain which greeted a film like *Flashdance*. I want now to suggest how the dancing welder in that Hollywood film can be used to comment upon the singing detective in the British television series. The film is transparently constructed around the principle of having something in it for all possible audiences. This activating principle may seem remote from the cultural debates and concerns which underpin the BBC production. It is, however, precisely this (commercially induced) drive to embrace contrasting social practices which provides the point of common contact. From this standpoint the film's very different solution becomes a means of pointing to what is specific about the *The Singing Detective* considered as discourse.

Flashdance is part romantic fairy-tale, part peep-show. The literary-derived conventions of a strong narrative line and of characters who possess some internal coherence are decisively undercut. The star is a women welder from a repressed religious family background who dances in a night club/strip joint and is practising to get a place in a classical dance academy. She resents her employer's sexual harassment but falls in love with him, asserts her independence but benefits from his patronage. She thus oscillates between such disparate role models as *Rosie the Riveter*, Gypsy Rose Lee, Rosemary Clooney and *Cider With Rosie*. And yet these inconsistencies are held in check by the narcissistic energy which the film generates, and which derive from its video-inspired fusion of popular music and visual images of dance. Like *The Singing Detective*, it therefore constructs, against the odds, a conception of the person. But unlike *The Singing Detective*, it constructs that conception not from the (male) mind but from the (female) body—and in ways which render the body as at once the subject of female action and the object of male gaze (cf. Mulvey 1975). The film therefore achieves that improbable integration of identification and objectification which its title implies. Thus 'Flash' denotes both the female subject's inner states (flash/backs) and a male audience's sexual pleasure (flash/flesh), and 'dance' is both an accomplishment to be identified with and a spectacle to be looked at.

Unlike *Flashdance*, *The Singing Detective* is grounded in a pattern of cultural debates and practices which gives priority to literary criteria. This is evident not only from the long list of books and plays adapted for television by the BBC, but from the status accorded to writers generally.

Thus in Britain the names Ray Galton and Alan Simpson (*Hancock, Steptoe and Son*), Dick Clement and Ian La Frenais (*The Likely Lads, Porridge*) and Johnny Speight (*Till Death Us Do Part*) were almost as well known as 'their' shows. By comparison, innovation in American television is linked to the production house (eg. MTM) or to the producer/director (eg. Stephen Bochco, David Lynch). Moreover, the dense intertextual referencing that is characteristic of innovative American television (now much accelerated through such series as *The Simpsons, Twin Peaks* and *Northern Exposure*) typically involves the invocation of other television programmes and films rather than books. *The Singing Detective*'s refusal of a visually and musically accomplished integration (*pace Flashdance*) is consistent with the British pattern of prioritising the literary. There is a routine interrogation or disruption of any presumption as to the veracity of the text's visual images. The consoling and integrating force of popular songs (of the 1940s) is nostalgically accorded full recognition *and* subverted.[6] Doctors suddenly become participants in a lavish musical entertainment, a nurse suddenly becomes a night-club singer, pyjama-clad hospital patients watch as a body is recovered from the river, an elderly candidate for a heart attack begins to sing like Bing Crosby. From the outset the text oscillates between disparate *mises en scene* which invoke *The Third Man* and the conventions of Jack the Ripper movies, war-time pin-ups, contemporary hospital dramas, family conflicts and images of community life.

Nonetheless such dislocations come to be understood as consistent with narrative integration and as the expression of the central character's own view of the world. For at the centre of this disordered pastiche is an author/patient (Marlow) trying to avoid death. His only power is in language, and this linguistic resourcefulness contrasts with, and is threatened by, his deteriorating physical condition and social dependence. What is signalled is a hierarchical ordering of the discourses within the text (childhood, detective story, hospitalisation), so as to privilege the position of Marlow-as-author/patient. The apparent narrative disorder is designed to ensure that the viewer, as bewildered as Marlow-as-patient, and as concerned to establish coherence, is moved to identify with his crisis. Apart from the off switch there is really nowhere else to go. This initial identification is reinforced through the accumulation of verbal evidence that Marlow-as-patient controls the activities of Marlow-as-detective, and through the accumulation of indications that Marlow-as-patient supplies and suppresses information about Marlow-as-child.

The text's narrative organisation is revealed as not so much linear as paratactic (cf. Richter 1974, p.17), i.e. dependent upon a circular structure so that the 'plot' seems to go round and round. Although it can, with hindsight, or on a second viewing, be reconstructed in linear terms, it employs a free approach to time, being structured more in accordance with the principle of progressive revelation than historical sequence. Far from being open, therefore, the text vigorously encodes a preferred reading. The viewer is drawn into the text as a problem-solving accomplice of its fictional author. As such, the viewer comes to recognise that the breaching of boundaries between Marlow's three worlds is a routine accomplishment. The absurd *can* be made to make sense (and what could be more absurd than the two villains in raincoats and trilbies, an Abbott and Costello duo who seem to have been scripted by Harold Pinter?).

Having firmly secured support for a narrative which privileges Marlow as a patient, all that remains is to kill him off. In this way the viewer can come to recognise the author of this achievement. Like the absurd, the happy ending thus makes sense. The operation was a success. The patient died but the author lives, the patient is shot but the author is saved—and by his own fictional creation. And secure behind him are the *other* authors of the text (the literate viewer and the production team), co-conspirators in the preservation of a threatened body of thought about culture in general and television in particular. The question which *The Singing Detective* raises is whether that body of thought is experiencing its last gasp or rehearsing a creative revival. If I am right, what is at issue is: Am I rite, or am I write?

In Britain, the culture of literary nationalism has had many forms of institutional expression, and has prided itself on having so assured a place. In those cultures, like our own, which have been so seduced by international images, its hold has always been more precarious. Yet if I am right, what the series signalled is that if a literary intelligentsia anywhere is to lay claim to credibility, it must constructively engage with television's massive cultural presence—and that in so doing it places its inherited assumptions and conceptual frameworks in crisis.

1 Quoted in James (1977, p.20).
2 In a programme in the *Meridian* series on BBC2.

3 The concept of '*auteur*' was originally developed by critics and film makers associated with the French film journal *Cahiers du Cinema*. It was instrumental in leading to a critical re-evaluation of hitherto neglected or devalued Hollywood directors and popular films. To vulgarise, the basic premiss was that by treating the film output of any given Hollywood director as a single entity for critical purposes, it was in some cases possible to identify the presence of individual artistry within the confines of an industrial system and the constraint of commercial imperatives. The cachet of *auteur* status was critically contested, being conferred only upon those directors in whose work it was possible to identify characteristic preoccupations and thematic complexities.

4 Esslin is an émigré anglophile, well known for authoritative writings on the theatre of the absurd, but unable to recognise that *Hill Street Blues* was not 'just a run of the mill police series'. He worked for BBC drama for many years before becoming a professor in California. Another instance of q.e.d.

5 After *Double Indemnity* Chandler not only worked in the film capital, but also wrote about it in undisguisedly hostile terms. The contrast with William Faulkner is instructive. Faulkner seemed much more sanguine about the differences between writing for films and writing novels, much better reconciled to the collective and commercial character of popular film-making. To judge from his letters, Chandler's opinions on Hollywood (and on television) did eventually mellow a little. See D. Gardiner & K. S. Walker (1962, pp.115–44).

6 Cf. the suggestion by Umberto Eco that postmodernism revalues the past 'but with irony, not innocently'. It is expressed in the attitude of 'a man who loves a very cultivated woman and knows he cannot say to her, "I love you madly", because he knows that she knows (and that she knows that he knows) that these words have already been written by Barbara Cartland. Still there is a solution. He can say, "As Barbara Cartland would put it, I love you madly"...(he) will have said...that he loves her, but he loves her in an age of lost innocence' (Eco 1985, p.67).

SEVEN

Flying by Nets

The Social Pattern of New Zealand Fiction

In the dominion of signs language neither reflects nor selects reality. It refracts it. Within the realm of print, how the world works becomes how words work. And if, in consequence, words are a route through which novelty can enter our social life, this is always in accordance with tacit controls integral to the medium of transmission. So language in all its forms is at once a prism and a prison, a means of scattering light and an instrument of social control. The opposition between these near neighbours in the lexicon is instructive. Their boundary is necessarily in contention. Because no fence can be built, the trace of their maledictions litters the very ground of their dispute.

The specific mode of representation determines just how this general difficulty is mediated. Put another way, how are authors to say what they mean, and mean what they say, when the conditions of communicability that are specific to literature preempt the range of possible meanings? In the writing of fiction this difficulty is not so much displaced as displayed in the decision to work within, but against, a pre-existing form, or in the effort to construct alternative forms.

This is a highly condensed and formal account of a complex and subtle process. It provides only the most elementary leverage on the difficulties which confront a given author or group of authors. If such a predicament looks familiar to writers in New Zealand, it also applies to such disparate cases as Jewish-American novelists of the 1950s, the 'new wave' British science fiction of the 1960s (cf. Perry & Wilkie 1975; Perry 1984), and of course the feminist literature of the 1970s. It is, however, just those texts which feature formal innovations or challenges which are of particular interest to sociology because it is the forms of fiction which are its content. There is something unnerving about the matter-of-fact way such interests are declared, and about the prospect of using so blunt an instrument as a probe. For sociology is purportedly hostile to detail; it has a built-in bias towards generality, a predilection for theorising, an anti-humanist tendency which can edge towards the anti-human. In its structuralist variant it even ratified the conceptual elimination of the human subject. The baby was defined by its bath water. The very idea of persons capable of reflexively monitoring their own conduct was subverted.

It is, therefore, not surprising that the contrasting conception takes such forms as '. . . the movement away from theory is a movement towards truth. All theorising is flight.' This particular example is the whimsy of an imaginary character in an Iris Murdoch novel, *Under the Net* (1954, p.92) but Rex Fairburn's hostility to Picasso provides a local counterpart. He claimed that: 'As soon as you abstract you falsify, and give the lie to life. . . . Hence the falseness of all abstract art, that is to say, of all analytic art' (Trussell 1984, p.119). In Pasternak's *Dr Zhivago* such sentiments take the shape of a critique of technical domination:

> Reshaping life! People who can say that, they have never understood a thing about life—they have never felt its breath, its heart—however much they have seen or done. They look upon it as a lump of raw material which needs to be processed by them, to be ennobled by their touch. But life is never a material, a substance to be moulded. If you want to know, life is the principle of self-renewal, it is constantly renewing and remaking and changing and transfiguring itself, it is infinitely beyond your or my theories about it. (Pasternak 1958, pp.305-6)

Whether English, or Russian or 'characteristically Kiwi'; whether whimsical or deeply serious or 'half-baked',[1] these examples exemplify the humanist project, in which an antipathy towards theory coexists with a respect for persons, for contingency, for particularity. Its adherents are deeply disturbed by a theoretically sanctioned contemporary rhetoric about the end of liberalism and the demise of the individual. Its leaseholds, even on the cultivated but marginal land of high culture, no longer seem secure. It is morally powerful but cognitively feeble. So its protagonists engage with theory much as Steinbeck's dispossessed farmer engages with the bulldozer which threatens his home. Like him, they confuse the proximate cause of distress with the effective one, and thus confuse a potential ally with a perennial enemy. It is true that the force which powers bulldozer and theory alike is property's progress, the changing social relations of the external world. But maybe the force is with you. The most pressing task of social theory is not to preside over humanism's demise, but to give sociological weight to its moral promise; to construct a conception of the person that is both possible within, and necessarily against, the limitations of our collective life. In its turn, what social theory stands to gain are some much needed lessons in subtlety.

Certainly my own purpose is not to clear the ground but to plant a marker. By locating a place (and creating a space) somewhere between Steinbeck's bulldozer driver and Kafka's land surveyor, I hope to avoid the moral indifference of the former and the cognitive indeterminacy of the latter. My claim is that there can be no flight from theory because there can be no escape from metaphor. Theory is explicitly grounded, or tacitly smuggled in, through this and other tropes.[2] Roger Horrocks (1984) has documented the aversion to theory characteristic of New Zealand's best-known critics, and singled out E. H. McCormick as exemplifying this tendency. Yet in McCormick's 1959 account of New Zealand literature the narrative is implicitly controlled through the use of organic imagery. Of the 1850s he observed '. . . the antipodean soil was to prove as congenial to the Victorian habit of poeticising as to those imported weeds which alarmed the settlers by their monstrous growth' (p.32). By the 1880s he had detected '. . . tiny and infrequent oases in a desert of facts, anecdotes, pointless descriptions, absurd melodramatic contortions' (p.49). In commenting on *Philosopher Dick* (published in 1891) he noted how 'the déraciné had begun to put down roots' (p.52) and located in the lines of Dommett's epic poem, *Ranolf and Amohia* (1872) some 'frail saplings in a forest of dead timber' (p.67). The writings of naturalist Guthrie Smith are viewed with special affection and allotted almost as much space (pp.98-102) as Katherine Mansfield. But then he is an author for whom *homo sapiens* is to be treated 'as a beast of the field' and a writer for whom Tasman's glimpse and Cook's landing marked the arrival of 'the seeds of death' (p.102).

Of the 1930s, McCormick writes:

> The growth of culture in a new soil is unpredictable; it follows no established sequence, it is subject to no universal law. All one can assert with certainty is that it requires time for germination and the indispen-

sable seeds of talent . . . the years ahead were to be the most fertile in New Zealand's literary history. . . . The requisite talent was present . . . (but) had revealed itself as yet only in obscure places or lay dormant, awaiting the necessary conditions for growth . . . the most fruitful literary decade of New Zealand's first century . . . produced a body of work which in an intimate and organic sense, belonged to the country. (p.108)

And of the immediate post-war period, he asks of the issues of *Landfall* under Brasch's editorship:

Again, nevertheless the carping, qualifying voice is raised: Need they have been so carefully pruned and cultivated? Could they not have found more space for the rank growth of experiment or the frail saplings of youthful self-expression? The answers must be in the negative. *Landfall* could only have been different by sacrificing its main source of strength, the principles of its editor. (p.139)

Throughout the text the tacit comparison is, of course, with the materialistic and the mechanical, as revealed in the critique of Julius Vogel's *Anno Domini 2000 or Women's Destiny* (1889), 'an elaborate product of the mechanism underlying the dreams of wealth and power . . . an orgy of mechanical speculation' (p.63). It is by way of this kind of contrast that such organic imagery routinely derives its plausibility and from which it acquires its coherence. Yet what leaks through the prose is not simply McCormick's debt to Leavis but the sense of a theory functioning at its limits, of imagery at the edge of its applicability. For if he appropriates the organic so as to sanction indeterminacy, he also discriminates against imported weeds and signals approval of landscape gardener Brasch.

Cultures are made. This is what McCormick cannot bring himself to say. It is what the present book has been at pains to say again and again. Cultures are no less of an accomplishment for being the product of work and interaction. Whether couched in the language of scientific laws or the imagery of literary criticism there remains an irreducible distinction between nature and culture, between the world and how we comprehend it. We are already, and necessarily, within language in the very making of such distinctions. That is where we are, and there we are both lost and found. Whether in science or art, the effort to confer a kind of facticity on culture, to imbue its conventionality with 'is-ness', is a conceit. In both mathematics and poetry, cultural production depends upon figures of speech. Both share a commitment to locating similarities amongst differences.[3] And it is down amongst those differences, amongst the details, where novel metaphors move and where new theories are built. Metaphor's movement is within that vital inch of space between prison and prism, between imagination and constraint, and theory's province is the construction of alternative interpretations of the world and the rehearsal of social possibilities.

As for the metaphor that 'all theorising is flight', it is itself a theory, albeit a paradoxical one. The paradox can only be resolved by abandoning the theory—or by re(de)fining the metaphor. The attractions of this second course of action have been anticipated by James Joyce. In a famous passage in A *Portrait of the Artist as a Young Man* he writes 'When the soul of a man is born in this country there are nets flung at it to hold it back from flight. You talk to me of nationality, language, religion. I shall try to fly by those nets' (1956, p.251).

Stephen Daedalus's commitment to such rhetorical flourishes may be very priggish, but there is also a residue of emancipation that is consolidated in Joyce's later work. The author of *Finnegans Wake* might even approve of the claim that sociology is, or more precisely, can be, a fly-by-net discipline. The net is a metaphor for theory. It is constructed in accordance with tried principles but flexible and dependent for its efficacy upon an appreciation of the particular stresses to which it will be subjected. The conditions of successful use are: an acquaintance with and respect for local currents; and the avoidance of premature closure. Since the net itself cannot escape from language, it too is part prison, part prism. It is both a form of control and a struggle to preserve meaning and to make sense. Its emancipatory purpose is the exposure of social constraints. A sociology which monitors conventional literary and linguistic usages, in order to identify their social function and the interests which they serve, places the emphasis firmly upon the imprisoning effects of language. And since it is often not events but language about events that is experienced, then the focus of such enquiry is typically on how words can succeed where policies fail (cf. Edelman 1977). It is not just that public utterances may have no determinate connection with the meaning of events. It is that the connection is effected not through meaning but through use. Control displaces meaning whenever the reader's (or listener's) need for symbolic reassurance coincides with the writer's (or speaker's) interest in providing it.

Such a combination may be strikingly impervious to every *reductio ad absurdum.* Thus the continuing ability to survive logical inconsistency has been a marked feature of the career of some well-known public figures. Within New Zealand the most dramatic recent example has been Ben Couch, but the exemplary case is undoubtedly the Dannevirke-born Joh Bjelke Petersen. Their political popularity simply could not be understood by attending only to *what* they said. Moreover, this phenomenon is not restricted to the realm of media politics. That it is a theme in our popular culture and our literature is suggested by Patrick Evans when he writes of '. . . the capitulation to perspectives and standards that derive . . . from what we believe the outside world believes of us' (1980, p.84). For Evans this both 'shapes our writing (and) also affects our judgement of what is written' (1980, p.71). In arguing for the critical centrality of a colonial/post-colonial distinction, he comes close to saying that it is not the words but the underlying social relations of dependence which endow our fiction with its sense.

When social function usurps meaning in this way the idea of a living language is under threat, but meanings *without* a social function cannot survive. This is consistent with Orwell's argument in *1984*, but allows for language being endangered not only by the novelty which he feared, but also by its absence. In New Zealand at least, it is the latter problem which has exercised commentators from Cresswell through Pearson to the group which gathered around the magazines *Parallax*, *AND* and *Splash* in the 1980s. One might say that three journals in search of a readership dramatised the paradox of novelty knowingly endeavouring to reproduce itself.

Patrick Evans, by contrast, is concerned not to make a tradition of the new, but to locate what is new in the traditional. Before novel meanings can be consolidated they must first be recognised. Hence his advancement of the cause of such writers as Ballantyne and Morrieson. They are seen as authors who reveal the slaughterhouse that 'is in our writing as in our hearts' (Evans 1980, p.84). What Evans shares with McCormick is a predisposition to contrast the organic and the mechanical, the arcadian and the butcher. What they also share is a tendency to use their preferred metaphors primarily as a means of critical *selection*. The burden of cultural *description* depends upon the presence of a contrasting image. Their respective evaluations are very different, of course. Evans makes an acerbic reference to 'a dream of rural gentility that never at any stage meant anything important' (1980, p.84), and there is nothing in his consciously polemical account which corresponds to Brasch's pruning shears. (There might have been, for as Lawrence Jones has pointed out [1982], the machinery of Morrieson's fiction is sometimes out of control.) What is of interest for my purpose are the cultural tensions which such conceptual dualism exposes. The common theme is that of being axed from the outset, 'split at the root', in Adrienne Rich's phrase (1983).

Kafka's *Metamorphosis* is an allegory on the intransigence of such concerns. It is a morbid story about a man who undergoes an involuntary change. He becomes a beetle, and the text is devoted to his/its efforts to comprehend and communicate that fact. By locating his protagonist between the no longer available and the forever unprintable, Kafka dramatises the experience of a particular kind of conceptual change, of having your ideas about the world go bad on you (cf. Gellner 1964, pp.50-64). The narrator's impossible task is to give an account of the experience of a beetle/man in the language of a man/beetle. Kafka tackles it by employing a recursive narrative that works upon its own premises. By shuttling back and forth between end states that are in turn unstable and untenable, he weaves a net that captures the mood of transition. The overall effect is of a form functioning at its limits, the feeling of being split.

What is it that makes a story written in German by a Czechoslovakian Jew so pertinent to the condition of fiction in New Zealand? Certainly the difficulties which Kafka's story dramatises are not randomly distributed. They affect some meaning systems more than others. Such systems are defined by the patterned relation between their concepts, and conceptual change is signalled by additions and deletions to the language in use and by the emergence of new meanings for old terms (in New Zealand the standard example is Christmas). Interpretations of, or for, the (New Zealand) here and now that are cast in the idiom of (Britain's) there and then, presuppose that all the terms remain relatively constant. If the changes are few or not strategic, then a combination of conceptual repair work, loose coupling and a tolerance for anomaly may obviate the need for overhaul. She'll be write. When, however, anomalies so proliferate that the relationship between received concepts and lived experience is fractured, meaning itself is a casualty.

Those concepts which act as a bridge between here and now and there and then are located in space and time. The forces which act upon them are not physical, however, but political and sociological. If the bridge buckles, the explanation does not lie in spatial or temporal dis-

tance *per se* but in the undermining effect of political and social transformations. For it is under conditions of *psychic* and *social* distance that
problems of literary expression and form are likely to be experienced
as both practical and pressing. The notion of estrangement and
the distinction between centre and periphery is *always* a matter of
attitude; it may also, but need not be, a matter of geography. Hence
Kafka's relevance to New Zealand writing. (*And* to Dennis Potter's *The
Singing Detective. And* to the way we read both.)

When such estrangement leads to formal innovations or challenges it
becomes of interest to sociologists. This methodologically induced presumption of relevance is, however, only confirmed if a text (or texts)
attracts co-practitioners who emulate or extend the form; cultural gatekeepers who advance the claims of a given text; some section of the
reading public; or any combination of these. On this view exemplary
innovations are distinguishable from idiosyncratic ones by their pattern
of social support, and individual accomplishment is gauged by the ability
to elicit such communal practices (cf. Kuhn 1970; Perry 1977). The
sociological test for whether one can fly by nets is the presence of a
supporting social network.

In the accounts of itself which New Zealand literature provides, this
linking of artistic achievement to communal organisation is best illus-
trated by the place which Frank Sargeson occupies. His early writing
offered a model solution to the social dilemma of a provincial intelligentsia. Here was a frugal, austere prose, responsive to the idioms of ordinary
New Zealand speech, in which the locals might recognise themselves.
And yet for the bookish it was manifestly literature rather than reportage;
it was made, not recorded. Accomplishing such apparent simplicity depended upon technical sophistication; for literary insiders such stories
worked through resonance, through indirection, through a predisposition
to read against the text. However different their own cultural agenda, the
makers of the Steinlager All Black commercial might therefore recognise
in Sargeson a kindred spirit. He offered a celebration of the local and the
ordinary, couched in a technically demanding form. Published in the
USA (*New Directions*) and the UK (*Penguin New Writing*), as well as
New Zealand, the stories prompted the admiration of critics, invited
emulation by others, and promised to confer legitimacy upon indigenous
literary practice both at home and overseas.

What helped make his solution workable was his recognition that the problem was conceptual. He had come to see his first attempt to write a novel as unsatisfactory because it was neither his own nor yet New Zealand's. The experimental short stories which he began to publish were efforts to construct a literary instrument that could be construed as both true to local conditions and yet aesthetically accomplished. It is therefore not surprising that his own account of his literary beginnings reveals a preoccupation with language, with form, and with the forms of language. As he put it:

> Was language merely the tool the novelist worked with, or was it a part of the raw material of life he worked upon, or was it a complex and difficult combination of both?
> . . . Then again, should it be the aim of the novelist to make the reader see, . . . or should one aim at writing sentences which appealed more to the reader's ear. . . . or should there be an effective blending of seeing and hearing? (Sargeson 1965, p.127)

This echoes the position in which Kafka places his protagonist but this predicament did not itself form the material of Sargeson's early fiction. It was a technical difficulty to be overcome rather than a cultural characteristic to be displayed; a personal trouble rather than a public issue. None the less Simon During's analysis of 'The Hole That Jack Dug' (1983) shows how traces of Sargeson's struggle can be detected in the narrative. What I take to be at issue is not whether 'it will stand', in Dennis McEldowney's words (1976, p.67), but whether the Sargeson *oeuvre* will bear the cultural load it has been obliged to carry. It is therefore not so much the original edifice as the condition of the platform which is the focus of attention. For, as McEldowney tacitly acknowledges, a later generation of critics must move in a very different world. It now requires an imaginative effort to grasp empathetically his earlier observation that

> I, too, believed that Sargeson's was the only possible kind of short story and his people the only true New Zealanders. This had not at all the emotional force of an *opinion*: it was something that *was* (cited in Rhodes 1969, p.168, italics in original).

This is both a testimonial and a confession, and what it reveals is the way in which Sargeson's early work bridged the critical distance between Ezra Pound's injunction to 'make it new' and Roland Barthes's sardonic claim that mythologies 'establish blissful clarity'. During's emphasis on the anoma-

lous as evidence of an aesthetic struggle within the text therefore becomes explicable as part of a larger social struggle around the text.
Sargeson's accomplishment is made problematic in order to recover the
generic problems he addressed. And since any such resolution of difficulties leaves a trace of the suppressed, this is where critical leverage is
exerted. The impetus for this endeavour parallels that which engaged
Sargeson himself, namely, the failure of the inherited conceptual equipment when applied to changed circumstances, as in the proverb which
Witi Ihimaera cites, 'The old net is cast aside, the new net goes fishing'
(1977). My own interest is not in rehearsing a commitment to the old
or the new but in weaving a net which can capture them both. In order
to probe the interconnectedness of artistic accomplishment and social
organisation, equivocation is more appropriate than adjudication. The
methodological premiss of such a stance is a view of Sargeson's stories not
as a topic but as a resource. The emphasis is not on textual criticism *per
se* but upon changes in community use.

The result is a shift of attention away from authorial intentions and
towards social effects; away from Morrieson's 'one of those poor buggers',
recognised after they are dead, and towards acts of recognition. The
central problem becomes that of determining what it is that a particular
work might possibly *mean* to the members of a given community. The
more traditional criterion, that individual authors may well have something to *say*, is not excluded, but it is contextualised. It is just because
individual texts both presuppose fiction as an institution and embody it
as a concept, that aesthetic pleasures are also sociological measures. From
this perspective the counterfactual truth claims of fiction are always socially sustained; an interpretative consensus is to be seen as an ongoing
communal accomplishment rather than a confirmation of transcendence.
Fictions, like funerals, are always for the living.

The socially constituted character of fiction is, however, routinely
repressed, decently buried for good and proper reasons. If the social ground-
ing of symbolic claims in this unexamined space were to be the focus of
attention, then they would never get off the ground. The possibility of art
depends upon the separation of literary from sociological problems. It is
by emphasising the former and neglecting the latter that both art *and* its
audiences, are created. Sociological inquiry therefore becomes aesthetically pertinent only when dominant assumptions are faltering, or when
competing claims jostle for pre-eminence.

What is involved is not just the tautological point that fiction, whether it is esoteric or popular, is made for an audience. Nor is it to replace an imagined ideal reader with a purely empirical conception—that would threaten to freeze fictional production into no more than a reflex response. It is to emphasise that audiences exist within a structured social field and bring with them an associated repertoire of expectations and beliefs. The literature of the absurd is a particularly instructive example, since absurdity has proved to be empirically unavailable, except as a qualifying adjective. When meaninglessness is *expected*, it is the social relations of literature which give it meaning. Through its sociology the absurd repudiates its own cosmology and as an ontological claim it therefore makes no sense! What it reveals is that fiction, in common with other established institutions, has a tendency to produce what Bourdieu (1977, p.164) calls the routinisation of its own arbitrariness.

This is too provocative a claim. If fiction is not the custodian of transcendence, neither is it wholly arbitrary. It is not so much that art is *a* lie which tells *the* truth (as Picasso would have it), but rather that Art is *the* lie which tells *a* truth. That truth is that fiction is sustained by convention and by interests. The tacit epistemologies and implicit structures which privilege given forms of literary activity depend not upon bedrock but upon consent, and this is more a question of social organisation than a problem of logic.

An exemplary work is thus forged from the interaction of a text and the audience which recognises it. In defining it that audience also defines and recognises itself. But the resulting interpretative consensus (i.e. an agreement about what is to be valued) is not the same as a consensus of interpretation (i.e. an agreement about the extent to which such values are present and the relative importance to be attached to them). It is this combination of individual choice and shared values which gives the micropolitics of literary communities their characteristic ambience and mysterious intensity. In the domestic disputes between the cultural gatekeepers and practitioners who comprise such groupings, nuance becomes essence. This is where insight sometimes resides. But only sometimes (cf. Gellner 1968, p.293). To the sociological outsider it is not the differences which are most striking, but the level of cognitive integration; not the diversity of the script, but the uniformity of the agenda; not the catch but the net.

Achieving such intellectual closure is a major social accomplishment.

It is that form of politics which makes art possible—and defines what form of art is possible. One way to measure the distance between these two points is by plotting Sargeson's path through New Zealand letters. His first collection, *Conversations With My Uncle and Other Stories*, appeared in 1936. The review of it in the *Press* of Christchurch, and the correspondence which followed, reappeared in Jean Bertram's contribution to the Sargeson *Festschrift* which *Islands* published in 1978. The review was brief, dismissive and anonymous. There were letters of protest from J.E.S. (Jean Bertram) and D.G. (Denis Glover), a rejoinder from the reviewer, a letter supporting the review from 'T.S.', and, finally, a note from Sargeson himself. What is captured by the sequence is the sense of a precarious literary community spontaneously mobilising its limited resources, at once constructing and defending itself.

Denis Glover invoked Jane Mander, Rex Fairburn and D'Arcy Cresswell in suggesting that 'Your reviewer gives evidence of reacting strongly to this general chorus of praise' (Bertram 1978, p.220). Jean Bertram comments that 'None of us had ever heard of T.S. and the Reviewer remains anonymous to this day . . . and it was some small comfort to reflect that the reviewer must be an outsider to refer to me as *him*' (1978, p.222, italics in original).

In such communities agreement on critical standards and shared criteria of competence are given expression and become persuasive not in general formulations but in particular aesthetic judgements. Critical disagreements are thus positively sanctioned on procedural grounds. They are seen as not merely inevitable but desirable inasmuch as they contribute to the refinement of aesthetic judgement and the consolidation of critical standards. The *Press* review implicitly challenged the presumption and the possibility of such agreed standards and thus the incipient rationale of a local literary community.

When such a critical exchange is reproduced in a collection of valedictory essays it acquires a rather different meaning. After forty-odd years a struggle to protect communal integrity has been sanctioned by events, it becomes a confident celebration of orthodoxy. Vindicated by history, the precariousness of that initial claim is filtered out. For example, *contra* Denis Glover, there is nothing in the original review which constitutes 'evidence' of reacting to the approval of other reviewers. It is the fact of non-approval itself which is treated as if it were evidence of such a reaction. And whereas Jean Bertram sardonically congratulated the reviewer on spotting the influence of Hemingway (and went on to impute jealousy as a motive), Sargeson's own contribution to the exchange made clear that his debt was not to Hemingway but to Sherwood Anderson. He added that 'I'd have thought that any decent reviewer would have picked this immediately' (Bertram 1978, p.221).

According to New Zealand literary mythology Jane Mander was amongst the more talented of those who fell victim to a hostile or uncaring local reaction. Sargeson did not. His persistence, against the flow of material interests, and in the face of social indifference, is also part of that mythology. What the *Press* episode anticipates is the gradual translation of Sargeson's individual endeavour into a pattern of communal response. For in 1932 the magazine *The Phoenix* had appeared. It signalled that the individual energies necessary to sustain a literature were present, and that the requisite forms of material, technical and social support, might perhaps be achieved. Despite its precarious economics (cf. Sinclair 1983, p.168), the journal did acquire a purchase on the idea of an indigenous culture. The establishment of a local branch of PEN in 1934, the series of New Education Fellowship conferences in 1936, were further indicators that not only were cultural aspirations beginning to expand, but so too was that fraction of the middle class which might consolidate them.

The form of Sargeson's stories cast these aspirations into fictional shape. They showed how democratic sentiments and critical standards might be made to meet, how local allegiances and transnational criteria of competence might be reconciled. Sargeson's stories worked at the point of intersection between communication and innovation, between a confirmation of the known and an affirmation of the new. They were accessible, but in a way that recognised that explicitness is the enemy of art. A year or so earlier Fairburn had anticipated that these might be the kind of stories which an artistically ambitious New Zealander would produce (Trussell 1984, p.145). For decoding them presupposed *knowingness*, a secret shared, a recognition of how difficult it was to write fictions whose surface was so unadorned. Like a plain black dress they were both democratic and exclusive, both flattering and demanding. What they made possible was a closet cultural elitism. Bill Pearson documented it in 1951 in that section of his 'Fretful Sleepers' essay devoted to New Zealand intellectuals, but its rationale had been made explicit by Fairburn in the 1940s. In *We New Zealanders* he had regarded formal support for democratic sentiment as perfectly compatible with 'the existence of an elite class or classes in a community; but such groups must base their authority on something other than the ability to sell commodities at a profit or the possession of lots and lots of sheep' (Fairburn 1944, p.22). That 'elite', 'class' and 'group' are viewed as interchangeable terms is analytically naive but ideologically appropriate. For by 1978 a literary community whose principle of legitimacy did indeed rest on 'something other' had consolidated its position. What permeates the Sargeson *Festschrift* of that year is the theme of an entire community congratulating not just Sargeson but itself. There is that same sense of too easily won satisfaction which our cultural critics find so unattractive when it appears amongst the populace at large. And this left-leaning right-mindedness is in celebration of an author whose earliest and most accomplished work characteristically sought to signal moral virtue through reticence and aesthetic merit through parsimony.

What this points to is the operation of a familiar political process and the attendant blurring of the distinction between social organisation as a means and as an end in itself. In this particular case it is displayed through displacement effects whose consequences are both sociological and artistic. Consider, for example, thickenings in the production of biographical musings, memorabilia and ephemera. The publication during the 1980s of Fairburn's letters, Sargeson's reviews and McEldowney's reminiscences were typical additions to the developing data base of an officially sanctioned and institutionalised aesthetic. They did make for a more reliable sociology; their contribution to art is much less certain. But then their formal content is less significant than their social function; they validate the past on behalf of the present. They are less about what 'we' were than about what their subjects have become. The tedium is the message.

Such a stylised contrast between solitary innovation and institutionalised orthodoxy, between the origins of a literature and its mature archival expression, falls some way short of explaining the transformation it denotes. But it does prefigure such an explanation. Furthermore the subversive tone of my remarks does have a constructive intent—that of opening up closure, of cutting the knot which binds the accomplishments of one period to the difficulties of another. For the irony is that the very social processes through which literary achievements are, and must be, constituted tend to create barriers to the recognition of subsequent artistic initiatives. Without such nets nothing can be caught, yet when a net closes nothing new can be caught. Until recently, however, New Zealand's high culture simply lacked that plurality of nets and that range of trawling grounds which might counteract the dangers of using aging but well-tried methods and equipment in the same favoured locations. For a writer who missed the net—and even for those who did not—the only alternative was to catch the boat.

And yet historically the impetus towards closure was critically appropriate, politically rational, and ideologically justifiable. In artistic terms it represented a considered attempt to rescue what was of value from the indifference of the wider society; politically speaking it was an apposite response to the economic and cultural marginality of the local intellectual life; as an ideology it was a conspiracy *for* the laity.

To understand this process of closure is also to see how and why the communal habits of a few came to be identified with the building of a nation. This involves probing the connection between institutional change and the ways in which literary intellectuals cast their nets. The latters' main trawling ground, in New Zealand as elsewhere, was that 'cultured' fraction of the middle class upon which an indigenous literature depends. The expansion of the university population is a useful indicator, not of the absolute numbers, nor even of the actual members, of this class fraction, but of its rate of growth. In Auckland, for example, the number of students in the period 1932 to 1942 wavered between 900 and 1200 but climbed rapidly thereafter. By 1946 the figure was around 3000. This was maintained until the mid-1950s when the next dramatic increase took place. By 1960 the roll had reached 4300. It had climbed to 5500 by 1965, and in 1970 it stood at 9300 (Sinclair 1983, pp.217, 245-6). Compare this with *Landfall*'s sales figures. Between 1947 and 1957 the number of subscribers varied between 632 and 817. It first achieved a four-figure subscription list in 1960 and first made a profit in 1965. By that time the print run was in excess of 1600 (Geraets 1984, pp.99-100). The possibility of a literary community (and a literature) of some consequence had first been signalled in the 1930s. Of the authors in *Speaking for Ourselves*, a 1945 anthology of fifteen stories which Sargeson edited, more than half would eventually produce collections of their own. By the end of the 1950s the New Zealand literary community had acquired a domestic constituency that was much larger than its own practitioners.

In reminiscing about his visit to New Zealand in 1948 Dan Davin

(1978, p.305) recalled both a distinctive camaraderie amongst local writers and, behind this stance, the reservations and rivalries characteristic of their overseas counterparts. That dilemma of participation and constriction which, as we saw in Chapter Two, Chapman (1973) and Copland (1973) interpreted as a distinctive feature of local literary method may therefore have been, in part, a textual refraction of relations within a small literary community. During the 1950s the aesthetic preferences of that community were marked by a certain focusing of attention, and the associated communal habits began to acquire an internal coherence. Not all at once and not without evidence of divergence (notably, for example, in the fiction of Maurice Duggan and the criticism of Monte Holcroft)— but in 1953 Sargeson's artistic and social importance was given public acknowledgment by an open letter to *Landfall* in honour of his fiftieth birthday. It was signed by most of the country's writers of fiction and, literally, conferred symbolic status upon both Sargeson and his work. The significance of this declaration lay in the fact that such a gesture was now *possible*. It was not the expression of an ideology but one strand from which an ideology might be woven.

The fabric of such a net was decisively thickened by two further strands. The first of these was Bill Pearson's 'Fretful Sleepers', written in London, but conceived against the background of the 1951 waterfront dispute. The second was Robert Chapman's 1953 essay on 'Fiction and the Social Pattern'. They expressed the frustrations of a handful of sensitive, intellectually ambitious individuals about the threat posed by conformity. The absence of an indigenous sociology meant that Chapman, Pearson and others combined the roles of ethnographers and cultural critics. The underlying tension in their essays was thus between descriptions that were sociologically adequate and prescriptions that were culturally feasible. This contrast was not so much resolved as *managed* by the emphasis on cultural homogeneity. The anxieties endemic to a mass culture perspective thus acquired a distinctively local inflection. Pearson (1962, p.348) suggested that 'local artists have a fear to appear in public without fulfilling every expectation of the audience, a craving for protective camouflage'. Olssen (1962, p.443) 'detected a sense of insecurity . . . expressed in a remorseless pressure to conform; so that we may not say exactly what we mean, nor demand exact meanings of other people'. And Chapman (1973, p.76) referred to a social pattern that is 'so homogeneous and hence so insistently demanding . . . that in order to see it, in order to write about it, it was necessary to escape'.[4] One effect of this preoccupation with the central features and centralising dynamics of our social life was to exclude just those counter-tendencies from which their own work derived.

These essays nevertheless opened a little window for a small section of an otherwise traditional middle class, providing illumination, fresh air and hints of escape. What was not anticipated is the way in which these defences against a social order which was alternately seen as indifferent and hostile would eventually become the ground for a collective project by an expanding 'new' middle class. Gordon McLauchlan's *The Passionless People* (1976) was explicitly influenced by Pearson's essay in its popularisation of the thesis that New Zealand culture and social life are deeply flawed. Whereas Austin Mitchell's earlier satire (1972) had been both sentimentally affectionate and intermittently astute, McLauchlan's polemical lumpen-sociology could be expected to appeal to those readers who saw themselves as exempt from the afflictions it claimed to document. The subsequent presenter of the Telecom share float, biographer of Allan Hawkins and author of *The Big Con* thereby foreshadowed the development of those formulae by which an emergent new middle class sought to wed condescension to populism. What began as artistic objections to homogeneity and a polemical cultural response to the political events of 1951 has been gradually transmuted into a social critique of egalitarianism. With the consolidation of its social and economic base, this process manifestly gathered momentum during the 1980s. What began as an attempt to enlarge and enrich New Zealand's dream of itself, thereby became an integral element in its repudiation. When Pearson had observed in 1952 that the New Zealander 'will not even sing as he feels . . . He is not so much singing as performing a tepid act of devotion to someone else's performance which is public property and must not be violated' (Pearson 1962, p.348), it had at least been partially offset by a muted recognition of local virtues. But the elements of the mass culture critique are all here, in bloom and waiting to be marketed.

This development was facilitated by a blurring of the distinction between works of fiction and matters of fact. I have said something of the critical reception accorded to Sargeson's stories by McEldowney and others. That reception encapsulated an argument that is central to Chapman's widely cited 1953 essay. In it New Zealand writers are viewed as ethnographers, texts are explored for the way in which they illustrate purportedly generic social processes. This is *one* way to practise the sociology of literature but it is no way to support specifically literary values. It allowed fiction to be pressed into the service of cultural nationalism by sanctioning the fiction that the dominant social realism was somehow factual— that literary truth and sociological truth somehow directly coincide. As in the histories which were soon to appear from Keith Sinclair and W. H. Oliver, the idea of nationhood was integral to Chapman's thesis. But whereas for a poet like Allen Curnow, New Zealand had to be invented (Curnow & Marsh 1945, p.2), and for a critic like McCormick (1959) it had to grow, for a historian-cum-social scientist like Chapman it had only to be discovered. In this version of literary politics literature, like politics, becomes the art of the possible. In his words 'Art and imagination lie . . . not in fresh creation after the imaginative uncovering of reality, but lie in the selection from this reality' (Chapman 1973, p.77).

In sociological terms the pattern of New Zealand life was seen as stable and homogeneous and the local literature at once described and evaluated this pattern by its mode of selection. A realist conception of literature was confirmed by a circular logic. To caricature: if there was no literature on the inner life of New Zealanders this seemed to imply that such a life was lacking. If there was no imaginative literature on the psychic and social diversity of small towns, this suggested that it was absent in practice. A. K. Grant (1984, p.38) has commented on how barriers to television satire were erected by such sentiments; to this can be added the specifically literary problems which Janet Frame and Ronald Hugh Morrieson were (eventually) to create for those habituated to such a way of thinking. For within a year of our best-known political scientist consolidating the New Zealand tradition in *Landfall*, our best-known living writer was decisively subverting it in Sargeson's garden hut. Which is only one reason why Janet Frame might also be called the best political theorist we have got. For it is, I think, important to insist that she writes not as a release from the world but as a means of apprehending it. This inverts the kind of conventional critical judgement of her as a gifted miniaturist for whom words are an escape. If I am correct it is no wonder that realist critics have trouble getting Frame into their picture of the world. They have painted themselves into a corner and it is, *pace* Wittgenstein, that picture which holds them captive. Neither Frame nor, as I shall shortly argue, a writer like Maurice Gee, seem bound by such constraints.

One consequence of this argument is that the very idea of 'the' New Zealand tradition is made both precarious and contingent—it becomes in every sense an indefinite article. This is detectable in the difficulties which beset a responsive critic like Lawrence Jones. At the beginning of the 1980s he began to posit the presence of not one but two New Zealand literary traditions. There are two because his logic is binary. The 'other' tradition is a residual category, defined by contrast with a realism whose central activating principle is the existence of a 'common phenomenal world' and whose focus is a 'shared common life' (Jones 1981, p.121). The argument rests on a distinction between inner and outer, between private and public, between subjective and objective writing which presumes, and therefore privileges, realism's epistemology. The problem is that such an epistemology can provide no warrant for Jones's claim that fiction in his 'other' tradition does have value. For value presupposes the representation of meanings that can be shared, that are somehow representative. The minimum social condition for such a critical judgement is that such meanings are not wholly subjective, but *inter*subjective, i.e. held by others.

Jones calls his essay 'The Inside Story', an appropriate enough synonym for the Trojan horse that it proves to be. For in order to sustain a distinction between an objective realism and a subjective other tradition, there are two preconditions. One must point to some group of writers or some putative audience for which the 'other' tradition is deemed particularly apposite. And one must identify how realism transcends such social factors—otherwise it too can be designated as (inter)subjective. Amongst practitioners Jones singles out the work of Helen Shaw and Russell Haley, bracketing it with the more experimental of Mansfield's stories, with Janet Frame's work, and the writing of Keri Hulme and Michael Morrissey. This small but disparate group consists of men and women, Maori and Pakeha, exile and immigrant, modernist and postmodernist, the young, the not so young and the dead. It is contrasted with Sargeson, Gee, Shadbolt, Davin, and Hilliard. Socially at least it is the latter grouping which appears as particularistic, as tightly integrated around commonalities of age, gender and (Hilliard notwithstanding) ethnicity.

It is, *of course*, the writing which matters. The point is that the presumption, and the presumptions, of realism can affect both the writing and the reading of texts. In the critical response to the Gee trilogy, for example, the enthusiasm for *Plumb* and the reservations about *Meg* and

Sole Survivor can be seen as shaped by the way the first volume confirmed, with great craft, realism's image both of itself and of New Zealand.
What was at once innovative and consoling about *Plumb* was the intellect of its central character. What is therefore all the more striking is that
Meg, set in the heyday of Michael Joseph Savage, provides no such
confirmation of what is still one of the most important of our national
myths, namely the first Labour government. By choosing to refract public
life through the eyes of a woman protagonist, Gee interprets this era
through the politics of the household. The resulting challenge to the
received version of that time is oblique, perhaps even unwitting, but real.
For as between the first and last volumes the central political question
which the trilogy poses is, how and when did we lose our innocence? The
premiss (and the romantic heart of our realism) exemplified by Plumb, is
that we had an innocence to lose. Sole is less consoling, at once more
attuned to the presence and the attractions of evil and more open to
moral indeterminacy and expecting less of others. The book's characters
resist unambiguous definition, they keep some part of themselves safe not
just from their narrator but from the reader. There is a sense of their
strangeness, of otherness. The form is looser, the narrative line more
meandering. The presumptions of a 'common phenomenal world' and a
'shared common life' seem less than stable. Rather what one sees is
realism at the edge of its applicability as Gee dips into the resources of
the 'other' tradition. As a result he perfectly captures the transformation
of liberalism from its position of being not merely muffled by New Zealand culture but baffled by it as well.

This is too brief an appreciation to do Gee justice. In advocating a re-
examination of *Sole Survivor* I want to do no more than suggest that what
we think about the writing may tacitly smuggle in some unexamined
social judgements. Patrick Evans both points to this process and engages
in it when he refers to 'our collective expectations of what a writer should
be like and how a writer should write . . .' (Evans 1981, p.31) and in
suggesting that 'we who care about fiction tend to do so because we have
certain expectations of ourselves and enjoy seeing these duplicated in
what we read' (1981, p.35). An invocation of a literary community and
a personal judgement, a persuasive definition and a formal analysis, are
all fused through the recourse to plural pronouns. And the 'we' who are
pointed to have 'our' sense of 'ourselves' reinforced, whatever 'we' feel
about Evans's analysis.

At the same time the activity of reading is more open and indeterminate than Evans's brief account of it allows. In fact, his own argument requires that he cannot mean what he says—although he cannot say what he means. He cannot mean what he says because to write at all presumes that readers can and do change their minds, change themselves—such change is the purpose of his article. And yet he cannot say what he means precisely because he is a member of a literary community whose conventions and received meanings are his own. In order to communicate at all he depends upon conventions that he seeks to change. It is not just the problem of how metamorphosis is to be accomplished, but how it is to be described *in order that* it may be accomplished. How do you tell a caterpillar what it's like to be a butterfly?

The difficulty with Evans's stance is that he is concerned not to comprehend metamorphosis but to determine its result. In contrasting Ballantyne's localism with Frame's internationalism, he sees the latter's pre-eminence and the neglect of the former in terms of a colonial/postcolonial distinction, as an expression of the cultural cringe. But what Evans, Jones and Gee all share is an awareness that the assumptions which have been taken to sustain New Zealand writing had begun to buckle, and that the pressures to which it was subject were not only from without but from within. In the mid 1980s, as in the 1930s, it was the fact of transformation which our most sociologically interesting literature grappled with and sought to convey. In what kind of society is the Gee trilogy and the Frame autobiography possible? How is it that a 'difficult' writer like Frame has produced three volumes in limpid, accessible prose and the Gee trilogy moves progressively from the moral and social certainties of Plumb into the murkier and indeterminate psychic territory of Sole? Why is it that these two projects move across one another as they do? In Gee the movement towards the present is also a movement towards reticence. It is not, however, the unwitting reticence of characters knowingly controlled by their author (as in Sargeson), but an argument for psychic autonomy, the creation of a liberal enclave. The main characters in *Sole Survivor* are all allowed some psychic space of their own, off the page. By contrast Frame's autobiography is less about difference, than about how a sense of difference is socially constructed, about the connection between social relations and a sense of self. This is New Zealand writing with the signs reversed. What was inwards has become outward, what was difficult has become clear—and vice versa.

Janet Frame has worked inwards from the edge of the alphabet, and Maurice Gee has moved outwards to the margins of realism. What they share is a distinctive form of peripheral vision. This derives not just from New Zealand's location at the edge of the world, or from the precarious social position of writers in the society. It is because they are outposts of that early warning system which a literature of any consequence represents. Such sentinels operate at, and sometimes below, the threshold of perception. They do not tell us 'what is there' as directly as realism implies. The premiss, and promise, of a sociology of literature is, however, that they *do* tell us. But if we fail to decode their message, then the prism of language may become a prison.

1   The references here are to C. K. Stead's observation on the enthusiasm of others for Fairburn, and to his own view of the man, in his *In The Glass Case* (1984, p.12).
2   The literature is now very large, but works by the philosophers Mary Hesse and Paul Ricoeur and the historian Hayden White are particularly relevant.
3   Compare Ezra Pound's 'Poetry is a sort of inspired mathematics' (1952, p.14), with Henri Poincaré's (1958, p.7) definition of mathematics as the art of giving the same name to different things, '. . . the recognition of likenesses hidden under apparent divergencies'.
4   Accounts from within the succeeding generation of intellectuals were marked by a shift in tone but by a continuity of concern, by greater security of tenure but not peace of mind. Thus Wystan Curnow's plea for the benefits of psychic insulation confronted a cultural and institutional infrastructure with 'a built in tendency to demand versatility . . . (so that the) chances are that the redundant instead of the rich, the reductively simple instead of the subtly complex, will prevail' (Curnow 1973, p.159).

EIGHT

Millennial Pursuit

From the *Listener*'s 'Man Alone' to *Theory K*'s Scout Troop

In *Being Pakeha* Michael King indicated that he had written his last book on Maori matters. In the film *Being There* Peter Sellers played his last part. It was the role of a good and simple man. He was a gardener; that was what he knew, that was what he did and that was what he could talk about. The plot centred on his unwitting entry into politics. In particular it was about the ways in which what he said about the nurturing of life, i.e. his gardening knowledge, was subject to reinterpretation by audiences and through frameworks which expressed very different priorities and interests from his own. What was meant to be taken literally was routinely understood metaphorically, because in the social contexts in which it appeared that was the only way it *could* be understood.

The link between these two works does not derive from their substantive content or subject matter. The connection lies in how each provides an incentive to understand the way in which cultural messages (whether autobiographies or gardening hints) are affected by changes in audiences and their priorities. This is no more than a sociological reworking of Wittgenstein's injunction to attend not to the meaning of propositions but to the uses to which they are put. Or to couch this point in less stark a fashion, cultural phenomena achieve their meaning only through their interpretation. From this perspective the response to *Being Pakeha*, like the response to the aphorisms of Sellers's gardener, becomes a kind of cultural barometer, an indirect way of charting discursive shifts and pressure points in the wider society. For example, the divergent treatment of King's book by the *Listener* and by *Metro* is, on this view, symptomatic of those wider differences to which the two publications give expression.

Let me develop this claim.

Jim Ritchie's *Listener* review of *Being Pakeha* appeared under the heading 'Writer Alone' (1985). A few weeks later, *Metro* staff writer Nicola Legat referred to the book and its author as 'flavour of the month' (1986). The two phrases are separated by rather more than their date of publication. They exemplify different modes of discourse and are grounded in divergent cultural assumptions.

Thus through its title the *Listener* review recruits book and author—without a hint of irony—to the long line of John Mulgan's heirs (and predecessors). In yet another reworking of Mulgan's well-worn theme of Man Alone, the 'facts' of Michael King's biography are wedded to the requirements of literary mythology—a mythology that has all but lost its power to persuade. A representative work of political liberalism is thus subsumed under a local version of romantic idealism. We saw in Chapter Seven how a generation of New Zealand literary intellectuals had found in the combination of literary texts and their own immediate social contexts a surrogate for empirical inquiry and a substitute for social theory. The result was a literature-inspired definition of this country that expressed the needs and preoccupations of a provincial intelligentsia. Whatever may have been its import for New Zealand writers, therefore, the Man Alone myth was always bad sociology. Good sociology can, to be sure, make for bad art, but better social research might at least have led to a *different* kind of fiction. It might even have contributed to the emergence of a social theory pertinent to local circumstances.

The substitute for such a theory was the Pakeha version of cultural nationalism and with it the argument that New Zealand was, in global terms, a special case. Keith Sinclair's history gave an inspired interpretation to this cluster of sentiments, casting them into a paradigmatic form (1959). The sentiments themselves continue to flourish, not only in the rhetoric of the state and the ideology of commerce but also in the minds of many New Zealanders. By the middle of the 1980s, however, the specifically cognitive components of this paradigm, had (like the Man Alone myth) all but run their course. Indeed what Michael King's experience suggests is that they had begun to go bad on their own adherents. Just as Sinclair's graphic account of Walter Nash's cap-in-hand round of Westminster and Whitehall (1976, pp.134–52) moved at the paradigm's external limits, so too did King's fine biography of Te Puea (1977) serve to point up its internal difficulties. Externally, the New Zealand state's capacity to regulate and minimise the country's vulnerability to realignments in the international division of labour could be seen to have been overstated. Internally, the capacity to regulate and reconcile social and cultural divisions could be seen to have been overdrawn.

Under the sign of cultural nationalism, Pakeha artists and intellectuals had been concerned to assert, and to construct, claims to local distinctiveness. As this gathered momentum during the 1950s and 1960s, there had been a marked tendency to cast Maori in a role given by the perceived shortcomings of the dominant culture (cf. Pearson 1974). The relative emphasis was on Maoridom as the repository of undervalued and unacknowledged virtues, rather than as the location for suppressed social and political rights. It was almost as if some kind of balance could be (or had been) struck between Pakeha material advantage and Maori cultural resources, between Maori spiritual wealth and Pakeha secular power. King's study of Te Puea moved within, but also against, assumptions of this kind, and probably helped realign their centre of gravity by a notch or two. As the Maori cultural and political revival began to gather momentum, it was, however, the appearance and reception accorded to Sue McCauley's novel *Other Halves* (1982) which can be said to have signalled a detectable shift in the perspectives of Pakeha commentators and 'opinion-makers'. This was not so much through the book's didactic account of bureaucratic practices, as in its combination of intimacy and otherness in the heroine's relation with her lover, and the way her assumptions about the terms of that relation are continually confounded. That a story constructed across divisions of age, class and gender, as well as ethnicity, was assessed and interpreted almost wholly in terms of the primacy of the latter distinction, was illuminating in itself.

This very schematic account of the high/middlebrow culture version of Pakeha cultural nationalism refers to an intellectual and artistic initiative which was consolidated during the 1950s and 1960s. These local practices may have expressed local specificities but they can nonetheless be compared in a fruitful way with initiatives that also date from that time but come from elsewhere. Thus although an imaginary meeting between an American novelist, an Italian film-maker and a New Zealand historian might seem like the preamble to an ethnic joke, it can be made to yield a moral or two.

The first point of overseas entry is the affirmative, but very partial and characteristically partisan, use made of the resources of black American culture (especially street culture) by Norman Mailer in 'The White Negro' (1957). In its metaphysical leaps and verbal excesses it deployed a style and tone that was, and is, many, many miles away from where we are. What was shared, however, was the strategy of challenging and revitalising the imaginative resources of the dominant culture, a strategy in which it was the perceived deficiencies of white America's culture rather than the priorities of American blacks which provided the framework of interpretation.

By contrast, Federico Fellini's film *The White Sheik* was a cool, satiric investigation of a much less sophisticated, but no less romantic, effort to break out of dominant cultural constraints. In this case the constraints were seen as those of provincial location. The film's focus was on a provincial couple confronted with the sophistication of metropolitan Rome. The husband exemplifies those petit bourgeois traits against which romantics revolt: routine, a surface piety, convention, respectability, support for authority. The wife follows her dream hero, the white sheik (a comic imitation of Valentino's own near-comic imitation, provided by a former butcher's boy and barber whose real name is Fernando). He becomes a creation not of flesh and blood, but of the needs of a romantic provincial living out, but not yet trapped by, a too narrowly circumscribed social and emotional life. If the specific cultural alternative imagined by Fellini's heroine sounds impossibly remote from New Zealand concerns, then both that inventory of constraints and the tactics for escaping sound all too familiar—'provincial dilemma', '(wo)man alone (with her dreams)', and a solution that exemplifies the problem it is designed to resolve.

Of course there are differences between American hipsters, Italian provincials and New Zealand intellectuals—and of course those differences do matter. A more developed argument would need to do justice to such distinctions instead of blurring them. What nevertheless seems to cause most unease amongst traditional liberals is the kind of theorising impulse which brings examples together in this way, without respect for their origin. That unease is both cognitive and social, in that it is partially conditioned by the frequency with which liberals themselves have been the victims of a theoretically inspired disdain for details. But liberalism's own besetting fault is the converse of this. It persistently confuses nuances with essences and local specificities with the *causally* efficacious (*sometimes* they are—the temptation to overemphasise these occasions is especially powerful for liberals who are also cultural nationalists). Both the unease with theory and liberalism's own theory therefore coalesce in those somewhat defensive passages in *Being Pakeha* which seek to set the record straight. But the truism that facts speak for themselves holds only within shared cognitive frameworks and it is, of course, the latter which have become (or come to be seen as) problematic. There is no place 'outside' of social relations from which those relations can be independently observed. It is this which rendered Michael King susceptible to a cognitive takeover from so improbable a source as a fading literary myth, and a socio-political critique from representatives of a resurgent people's movement.

It was suggested in Chapter One and argued in Chapter Seven that the Pakeha-derived version of cultural nationalism had been conceived and developed in *opposition* to the dominant tendencies in the wider (mass and popular) culture, and had purportedly been intended to discover and celebrate the indigenous and the individual. Yet in so doing it effectively replicated high culture/mass culture distinctions and assumptions derived from metropolitan centres. This particular pattern of opposition and commitment rendered it vulnerable to the challenge that its forms (including its individualising tendencies) are both colonial and colonising. This has left it much less space in which to play, and by the mid 1980s it had become much more diffident in its reviewing practices. As a high-cultural solution to nationalist aspirations it is crippled by guilt and can no longer be made to work. At *this level* it looks set to be displaced by Maori culture, in which the relevance, relations and tensions between high-culture position and folk, mass and popular cultural forms are clearly both different and unexplored.

By contrast *Metro*'s acerbic remark about 'flavour of the month' moves in yet another register, cashing in on the language and practice of marketing. This is not beleaguered liberalism under fire, but an ascendant social tendency refracted through a prose style which congratulates itself on its own cynicism. It is therefore not the argument which is so unattractive, but the tone in which it is made. It occurs in the context of an article on the Maori nationalist group Te Ahi Kaa, in which the very inchoateness of *Metro*'s interpretation signals something important about the magazine's ideology and its success. In brief, to read *Metro* as internally inconsistent (i.e. from a traditional liberal perspective) is, I will argue, to read it from a cultural stance outside that of the audience to which it most appeals.

The appropriate starting point is the *look* of the magazine rather than its prose. *Metro* is routinely referred to as Auckland's 'glossy'. That is one way to describe a thin covering which nonetheless transforms that to which it is applied, and through which disparate subjects are rendered less heterodox. The look is not, however, simply the result of a shiny paint job, but of an approach to magazine production in which design criteria occupy a strategic role. One consequence is that its features and many (but not all) of its adverts participate in a shared aesthetic. It is an aesthetic in which the flow of influence is in both directions. For *Metro* has both induced a different type of magazine advert in this country and itself been influenced by advertising canons. It is not so much that *Metro* is integrated by its adverts as that the adverts are integrated into *Metro*. Throughout the 1980s the contrast with the *Listener* was striking, going well beyond those expected differences which derive from price and frequency of publication. *Metro's* visual representations exemplified a much more unified semiotic. The older magazine's prose features clearly signalled their enclave status through their black and white photographs and a typography that contrasted with the surrounding adverts. Throughout this period the *Listener* sought to bracket off and to privilege the printed word, to distance it from the market, to repress its commodity status and thereby both signal and amplify liberalism's cultural space.

In *Metro* the connotations of the visual imagery are of pleasure, of consumption and of their mutual interdependence. Commodification is not repressed, but celebrated; the prose is not only contained within, but also contained by, the magazine's format. Inasmuch as *Metro* is a 'marketplace for ideas' they are clearly inscribed in a commodity form—this is the terrain on which Felicity Ferret's gossip and Bruce Jesson's politics could be made to meet. The magazine makes some use of ideas and intelligence but, like its central constituency, it does not value them for themselves. They are incidental benefits rather than integral elements. This is because *Metro* can provide no basis for distinguishing between cleverness and intelligence, between the notion of a celebrity and a person of substance. Its own primary allegiance is to a cleverness whose defining characteristic is its compatibility with markets. On a television programme in the *Close Up* series during 1986 it was therefore possible for Gordon McLauchlan (himself a *Metro* contributor) to be

LIVELY ARTS
A NEW FACE IN THE GALLERY

ACAG director Christopher Johnstone: "I'm the least arty person you'd expect to find."

PETER SHAW

CHRISTOPHER JOHNSTONE is the new man at the Auckland City Art Gallery. He's 40, an Australian educated in Ireland and England, speaks French and German, and is interested in dance, ceramics, motorcycling, walking, swimming, sailing and tennis. Those who find it important will be relieved to find that he loves watching sport on TV and actually attended the Auckland/Wellington game at Eden Park. "I'm the least arty person you'd expect to find," he says.

From the look of his CV he's spent a great deal of time working very hard over the last 15 years. He came to Auckland from the Art Gallery of South Australia where he was manager of public programmes; before that he was assistant director of the Art Gallery of Western Australia and before that, curator of education and information at the National Galleries of Scotland. His first major appointment was as research assistant at the Tate Gallery's modern collection. The impressive list of exhibitions, projects

and publications with which he has been associated takes up 11 closely-typed pages.

Like his predecessor, Rodney Wilson, Johnstone believes that sponsorship is quite essential to the gallery's operations. However, he is also aware of the pitfalls.

"Ever since I was first involved with the promotional side of projects I've been aware that you mustn't over-promote. And there must be no compromise of aesthetic or artistic control just because a show is being sponsored. People must hear about our exhibitions but they must not be disappointed by too much promotion. It can have severe repercussions on attendances at future shows.

"Our main thrust is always to be as many things to as many people as possible. Over the next few years we'll earmark specific areas of the community to develop and communicate with. The elitist come-and-get-it-if-you-want-it is certainly not my view. Our art is elitist, it can be obscure and complex, but there is always something here that is accessible."

Johnstone believes that promotion

experience. He recalls the difficult job he had in promoting a major Poussin show in Edinburgh. "I briefed an agency on the problems involved in getting people into such a difficult show. They came up with a humorous, even joky campaign which succeeded in creating a surprising awareness. The paintings were as rigorous and difficult to deal with as any art but the interpretative material was lively, interesting and affordable."

JOHNSTONE'S FIRST task at ACAG is the production of a clear set of publishable policies about how the gallery functions and where it is going in terms of exhibitions. "We should publish our policies so that a level of debate in the community can take place. The feedback is of great value to us," he says.

"There is much criticism and misunderstanding of the role of heritage institutions and a lot of it comes from the lack of published documentation."

Immediate plans for the collection are all based around documentation. Johnstone thinks that there should be a greater

DEBORAH SMITH

consistent in describing the magazine as 'venal' and 'meretricious', and subsequently go on to say that he liked it. Faced with that initial judgement, editor Warwick Roger observed without acrimony that 'Gordon is entitled to his opinion'. What was implied but left unsaid was '. . . but the market decides'. What was affirmed by both men was *choice*, but choice as mediated through commodification. Hence Warwick Roger's laconic observation that '*Metro* is purchased by Ponsonby social workers who hate it and white collar Pakuranga residents who love it'. What is most interesting is not the marketing stereotypes or the use of the 'does it sell?' criterion, but the sense that Roger views *both* groups with some disdain. It is as if his conception of an ideal readership is one able to distance itself from the magazine, to view it with some equivocation.

This seems to me a response which is also signalled by the magazine itself. Thus *Metro* is at its most confident—and at its best—when puncturing that aura of sanctity and piety that marks off some forms of public commentary in this country. This sort of critisism appeals not only to the selfish and the cynical, but to decent people who need to see themselves as worldly. (The term decent even has an archaic ring to it—it is both liberalism's special strength and the basis of its vulnerability.) But because the magazine lacks any standard of seriousness that is independent of the market, it lacks a language through which worldliness and selfishness might be prised apart. One result is that any attempts to transcend those limits (such as the more unctuous of the editorials) read either as inauthentic or as parodies.

The Nicola Legat (1986) article on Te Ahi Kaa illustrates a related tendency—a prose style divided against itself; one which asserts the seriousness of its message and then moves to subvert it. This expresses a dual—and potentially contradictory—imperative, that of locating problems for readers whilst yet furnishing them with controlling definitions that are consistent with the existing order. Thus in the same article in which Michael King is designated 'flavour of the month' there is a reference to Atareta Poananga 'taking up Michael King's challenge—though her rejection of him would never let her express it in those terms'. And the account of her biography which the article contains is headed, 'What's a girl like you doing in a place like this?' (It's not clear whether *Metro* dropped the adjective 'nice' by accident, or because of a failure of editorial nerve, or because it wanted to obliquely convey a judgement on Ms Poananga to its readers, or because it doesn't know enough, or because

← Textual symbiosis: facing pages from *Metro*'s June 1988 issue showing the magazine's unified aesthetic.

it was slightly ashamed of a cheap shot, or because it was typographically convenient.) The point is not simply that *Metro's* grammar is that of consumerism, but also that, in Sapir's phrase, 'all grammars leak' (1921, p.35). For all its apparent brashness and confidence, *Metro* routinely points to the limits and uncertainties of the world view from which it derives its sustenance.

The contrasting trajectories of these two magazines during the 1980s is, on this view, explicable as an aspect of the rise and fall of contrasting discourses. This in its turn was linked to the emergence of those divisions within the middle class through which New Zealand's changing relation to the imperatives of the world economy were mediated. The salient distinction was between that section of the middle class which saw its position, interests and prospects as dependent upon the umbrella provided by the nation state, and that section which saw its position, interests or prospects restricted or threatened by that state. In practice, any given grouping within the middle class could always be expected to be ambivalent about its relation to this distinction, whether for opportunistic or altruistic reasons. But the general tendency which gathered momentum during the 1980s was a mutually reinforcing combination of a reordering of the country's location within a global web of dependencies; the expansion of an externally oriented fraction of the middle class; and the elaboration of a discrete, market-vindicating form of discourse. During this time the *Listener* presided over the secular decline of a print-based, high/middlebrow cultural nationalism, a nationalism purportedly exemplified in the policies and institutions, sustenance and sponsorship of a (grudgingly) benevolent state. *Metro* by contrast was at once congruent with, and constitutive of a more sensate, image-oriented and market-based pattern of cultural development.

But notwithstanding the hollowing out of the specifically *cognitive* content of cultural nationalism (associated with its high/middle brow version), the sentiments associated with popular nationalisms continued to flourish. Class, ethnic and gender conflicts may have proved more intractable than the cultural nationalist thesis of New Zealand exceptionalism could accommodate, but the yearnings that it had (indirectly) addressed were undiminished, accelerated even, by such evidence of division. Such culturally powerful dispositions frustrate attempts at cognitive clarification. For under nationalism, what gets transformed into destiny is not biology, but chance (Anderson 1983, p.19). Nationalist sentiments are nevertheless constitutive elements of personal identity for their adherents. This provides a continuing powerful emotional incentive to look for a haven in which they might flourish, especially if, as in New Zealand, their traditional cognitive basis was fracturing. What was expanding during the mid 1980s was the market and its associated mentalities. At the time, therefore, it sometimes seemed as if casino capitalism, the stock exchange and Gordon Gekko 'wanna be's had all but displaced more traditional aspects of popular culture as a locus for nationalist feelings and beliefs.

It was in this context that a management textbook called *Theory K* (1986) became a local publishing event, a runaway bestseller which celebrated, both on and between its covers, such now defunct companies as Equiticorp and Chase.[1] As with Telethon, the puzzling question is how could its improbable combination of nationalist sentiment, market principles and corporate rhetoric actually make sense? And, as with Telethon, the answer is dependent upon a method of reading which goes beyond the formal characteristics of the work, and attends to the circumstances which produced it and to the condition of the audience which recognises it. This is why reviewing it for the *Listener* (as I did in early 1987) proved to be such a curiously disorienting experience. The book itself was a mess, conceptually inchoate and based on a research design that I would have failed if it had been submitted as an undergraduate essay, let alone as an application to an official agency. Yet it had attracted $38,700 in research funds from the private sector, been written by four (mostly senior) academics, three of whom were acquaintances of mine, and had been duly lionised by Auckland University's public relations office. It had also been linked to a lavish New Zealand-wide corporate awards ceremony at Auckland's Regent Hotel, sold like the proverbial hot cakes and acquired a seal of approval from sources as disparate as Gordon Dryden and Roger Kerr. In brief, what was signalled was that the proper object of investigation was not so much a particular book as that wider social pattern in which it was implicated. When the *Listener* review finally appeared, I was buttonholed on campus by individuals both known and unknown to me, whose general message was 'Thank God, somebody has actually put into print how bad a book it is'. That such a work was not only possible, but that it had become a commercially successful cultural icon, seemed to speak to, and to speak for, some larger social transformation. The review as originally published was largely given over to the identification of methodological and conceptual problems, but it also touched on the manner of its reception. It is reproduced below not (or at least, not only) because it has worn better than its subject, but because it is a necessary preamble to *another* way of reading the book. This second reading recruits it to that realm of myth and magic, fairy tale and fantasy (with which Chapter Two began and) where it rightfully belongs.

Theory *K* is explicitly indebted to Peters and Waterman's *In Search of Excellence*, a book by two American management consultants which appeared almost five years ago. Almost five hundred years ago the Renaissance scholar Erasmus wrote a satirical essay called *In Praise of Folly*. Both works were runaway successes, for both offered highly readable but serious advice to those ambitious for wealth and anxious for power. Both were critiques of orthodoxy, whether in the shape of American business school education or medieval scholasticism. Both were also the work of insiders. Thus *In Praise of Folly* can be read as an exercise in blowing the whistle on organisational and ecclesiastical politics. And Peters and Waterman's nominal data base of executive interviews seems less important than their reliance upon those more tacit forms of knowledge which come from continuous association with the subjects of research. What they share with *Theory K* is the dramatisation of a triple problem. At issue is: the methodological puzzle of how to acquire reliable knowledge of organisational behaviour; the literary problem of how to present it in an accessible form, and the ideological question of how (and to whom) to present it in an acceptable form. I want to comment briefly on how these factors intersect in *Theory K*.

The book's basic finding is that successful New Zealand companies have distinctive organisational cultures, presided over by visionary and enthusiastic leaders. Despite its passing resemblance to the (Jim) Jonestown theory of management, this is an interesting working hypothesis. Its presentation as an established datum is, however, derived from research procedures which lack adequate conceptual or methodological controls as a means of detecting error. Let us accept (for the moment) that it is OK to rely on leading business people to provide an initial assessment of what constitutes well-managed outfits. (Noting only that this increases the likelihood of excluding public sector organisations—such as Treasury—as well as such institutions as Playcentre and such initiatives as the Kohanga Reo programme.) Having identified a few companies in this way, the list is then amended and extended in the light of data on financial performance and various ad hoc criteria. The next step is to interview the relevant chief executives. The highest paid managers and employees at given levels are also interviewed, using a questionnaire which opens with a query about why do they think that this company was selected as an example of excellence. The students doing the interviewing are required to write a report which forms part of their assessment for degree purposes. Finally a composite model is constructed from the results of this process. No company is taken to be exemplary, but rather some of its practices are identified as forming part of what excellence might mean. This model is then used as a benchmark against which organisations can be assessed.

At each stage, therefore, selectivity and filtering take place in ways which are likely to have cumulative rather than random effects. The general questionnaire reads like that American newspaper that prints only the good news. The advice to students on how to write their reports requires them to include at least four stories which 'bring to life the points in your summary'. There then follow examples of what such stories might look like ('innovative thinking, major success, legend about customer service, effective supervision, inspirational leadership, total commitment'). The logic of the research design is thus circular, an exercise in persuasive definition. Its findings are best understood as a combination of what the authors would like to hear, what the interviewers think they want to hear and what the interviewees would like them to hear. This is survey research without its usual methodological controls, and cultural anthropology without its detailed investigation of context. What it blurs is the crucial distinction between official rhetoric and typical practices.

From the outset the text is marked by internal inconsistencies and otherwise suspect generalisations. On page 3 the authors bemoan the overcontrol of New Zealand organisations and see this as linked to the dominance of accountants and lawyers on company boards. Yet before long they are waxing enthusiastic about companies like Chase. By page 7 they have managed to recruit opponents of the 1981 Tour and Bob Jones to the same side (the new consciousness of the eighties). And page 9 suggests that both teamwork (in soccer) and individualism (in cricket) are not rival tendencies of action but examples of excellence. The important question for managers is thus which game are they playing (i.e. what are the options, and under what circumstances does a given course of action work best); what the authors tell them is that they approve of winners.

This conceptual looseness is the basis of the book's ideological possibilities. For it suggests that companies as disparate as L. V. Martin and Equiticorp nonetheless have a distinctively local form of management in common (there is, after all, a sense in which a silver fern and a silver Mercedes resemble each other, and the book can be used to legitimate the latter in the name of the former). The disclaimer that this is not an academic text will not do, for the authors trade on their university affiliation, not least by trading off their students' labour. The laudable aim of producing an accessible and entertaining book should be an incentive to clarity, not a licence for loose thinking.

The book's literary style fuses the ideological message with commercial appeal. The number of italicised words is one indicator of the level of hype—my sample suggests an average of around four per page. The prose itself reads like *Jane Fonda's Workout Book* interwoven with extracts from a Mills and Boon romance, i.e. it alternates between breathless and deathless. The parallel with romantic fiction lies not so much in the theme of 'Could He Be The One? (though there is some of that) as in 'Could This Be The Way?' Hence all those italics.

Possibly the most instructive thing about *Theory K* has been its (un)critical reception. We may have swapped old orthodoxies for new ones, but it is still the silences in our public life which speak volumes. The channels for criticism are few and sustained debates infrequent. It is a situation that Erasmus would have recognised. And he might also have recognised that although *Theory K* consciously starts off in search of excellence it unwittingly ends up in praise of folly. Perhaps that's why one of its authors' favourite stories (p.64) is about a boy scout troop with the wrong map.

Like the original review, my second reading is designed to put *Theory K* in its place. In the *Listener* version, that place was unequivocally a 'fail' grade on the scale of reliable knowledge. The second reading continues to depend upon a recognition that the book displays the surface appearance of social research without its substance. But instead of emphasising *Theory K*'s distance from sound methodology, attention shifts towards its closeness to, and affinities with, some rather different social practices. They are the otherwise devalued and belittled activities of reading women's romantic fiction and embracing the situational logic of Melanesian cargo cults. This kind of observation usually begins, and ends, as nothing more than a throwaway line in faculty gossip, but it merits being pressed somewhat beyond that point. When such activities are interpreted with more sympathy and less condescension than I managed to muster for *Theory K*, or believe that it deserved, then they can provide insights into the social meaning of fantasies in general and managerial ones in particular.

That managers not only have, but need a fantasy life is a function of the indeterminacies of their occupation. At the most general level there is the gap between on the one hand, the synoptic rationality of classical management theory, the secular theology of corporate strategy, the priestly litany of mission statements; and on the other, the messy contingencies, micropolitics, cock-ups and moral mazes which is their day-to-day experience. More substantively the rhetoric of 'management as a profession' confronts jobs that in practice are: heterogeneous in their tasks and knowledge base; resistant to either codification or occupational control; vulnerable to hierarchical pressures, internal limitations and external constraints; subject to internal differentiation and stratification. Under these circumstances the function and appeal of a book like *Theory K* is precisely analogous to the function and appeal of romantic fiction. It transports the reader from the realm of everyday experience to another, mythical place. Thus the respondents in Janice Radway's *Reading the Romance* (1984) experienced the act of reading itself as a means of symbolically removing themselves from the demands of a situation in which they were characteristically expected to nurture others. When reading romances those demands were (briefly) suspended, and it is they who were (vicariously) nurtured. In like fashion, my suggestion is that for managers to read about how success is attained is to tacitly participate in constructing the very (problematic) idea of management and to (vicariously) experience success. Such texts therefore move at, and are used to work, the gap between the rewards promised by dominant discourses (i.e. emotional fulfilment and occupational success respectively), and what is actually experienced by their subjects. In each case there is a renewal of motivational resources, achieved through and with that reassurance and confirmation of the subject self which comes with the act of reading the text.[2] Where, as in the USA, this rhetoric is of long standing, management recipe books jostle alongside diet and exercise programmes on the bestselling lists, forming part of a more general pattern of work on the self.

Radway's women readers recognised that the texts were fantasies; neither their own lives nor real men were as portrayed in the stories. But for them the opprobrium conventionally attached to the notion of escapism was absent. Such reading was, in context, experienced and interpreted as an affirmative act, a way of saying 'this is my time'. By contrast, a management text such as *Theory K* is supposedly not about escaping controls but about exercising them; such works purport to walk along the wall between fact and prescription. *Theory K* may have been cognitively feeble, but it was both rational in intent and oriented towards change. Its social meaning and effects are therefore not limited to its immediately therapeutic function for individual readers. It was also a millennial dream in action, and as such it spoke to a larger structural transformation. Such millennial pursuits characteristically draw upon a society's common myths, dreams and background beliefs, promising to realise them through easily understandable methods and with the material resources that they have.

Melanesian cargo cults are a distinctive form of such millenarianism. In Jarvie's comparative account they are seen as arising in small, closed, economically, politically and culturally homogeneous societies which are suddenly subject to disruption and change by external agents (1964). The latter may either actually take over the society, or at least behave authoritatively, or are rumoured to do so. They are wealthy, successful and powerful but they do not behave in accordance with local conventions. They are not therefore interpreted as *morally* superior. Locally the problem is how to get their kind of wealth, power and success. Cargo cults are attempts to grasp the techniques through which such valued goods and resources can be acquired. Such attempts are, however, constructed from within the existing local framework of knowledge and belief. Indeed, they have to be in accordance with that framework if the cult is to attract followers (in Worsley's view such cults are incipient nationalist movements [1957]). Observations of these external actors are rendered intelligible in relation to the already existing categories of understanding. Cult behaviour thus mimics the surface appearances of those outsider practices that are seen as associated with the generation of wealth, power and success. This frenzied pattern of activity fails to produce the goods. With this failure a *particular cult* may collapse but *not the magico-religious explanatory framework* (Jarvie 1964, p.119) which underpins it. This can lead to an accelerating sequence of cults, each briefer and more desperate than its predecessors.

Theory K emerges out of a New Zealand undergoing its own rather more secular variant of such a transformation. A predominantly closed domestic economy, sheltering behind the wall of tariff controls and under the umbrella of import substituting industrialism, rapidly gave way to one open and exposed to international competition. The contrasts were of course less striking, and the response less dramatic and less apocalyptic than in the more obviously 'classic' instances of millenarian movements.

But the latter none the less offer parallels which seem more than merely fortuitous.

We have seen that the authors of *Theory K* filter a reading of Peters and Waterman through the pre-existing language of cultural nationalism, but take their title from Ouchi's *Theory Z* (1981) (derived in its turn from McGregor's Theory X and Theory Y [1960]). They incorrectly claim that Theory Z is 'a label for the successful managerial model used by large Japanese organisations' (Inkson *et al.* 1986, p.21). It isn't. Ouchi's book focuses on American corporations, and Theory Z refers to that ensemble of practices within US companies which purportedly combine elements of Japanese and American management. This is an instructive error. The commercial success in the USA of books like those by Ouchi and Peters and Waterman was expressive of a developing preoccupation in the American management literature with Japanese competition and success, and a distinctively American explanation of it and response to it. That explanation and response took the form of an emphasis upon the significance of 'organisational culture'. This is in striking contrast to that scholarly literature on Japanese business written by Japanese and Japanese-speaking academics which places much more weight on such institutional factors as the specific configuration of large firm/supplier relations, the position of finance capital and the pattern of state/economy linkages. *Theory K*'s own emphasis on 'organisational culture' replicates this American preoccupation but fleshes it out with some local content and conventional nationalist sentiment. A concept which, in its original formulation, was already required to do far too much work thereby acquired yet further responsibilities. In its nationalist garb the concept came to serve as a substitute for resources, a pre-existing, free, yet precious commodity waiting to be mobilised. In its cognitive guise it came to serve as a substitute for explanation, the perfect residual category into which can be bundled whatever is not otherwise accounted for. In its prescriptive role it came to serve as a substitute for inquiry, the basic parameters having already been given by the Peters and Waterman text.[3]

Theory K is a university product. As such, the book also says something about that institution and its changing pattern of internal and external relations. I have already signalled a methodological objection to using the product of unpaid student labour as both a source of data and as a means of student assessments (i.e. that under such conditions, reports are written so as give examiners what the writer thinks they want to see).

This matter-of-fact use of students is, however, also symptomatic of a different order of problems. For no matter what the methodological implications may be, there are overriding moral issues involved here, and with them the integrity of the university as a liberal institution.

One of the many measures of our present troubles is that this kind of terminology has come to seem overused and overblown. The very notion of a principled public language has been severely damaged if not permanently discredited. Cynicism makes more sense. It has therefore become more difficult to find a form of words through which a wider, and not obviously self-serving sense of unease about the universities can be conveyed with conviction. Yet New Zealand is not (or at least not yet) Thatcher's Britain in the extent of its hostility towards the cultural achievements of the liberal university, nor so inimical to its guiding myths. The university persists as an idea and as an ideal, and one can, in general, point to the continued resilience, resourcefulness and basic decency of most academics. But here, as in Britain, we have almost all learned how to trim a little, how to hustle a little, how to get by and go along, how to routinely give that much more weight to questions of expediency. These tendencies are at work throughout the tertiary system. It is, however, within the business-school milieu that the present dilemmas of the liberal university are most clearly dramatised and its future is most clearly being played out. For it is in the business schools that there is the most direct confrontation between work of real quality, pure hokum and less than pure opportunism.[4] And it is in the business schools that that confrontation most matters. Such a contest expresses rather more than the perennial manoeuvring of university politics and involves something other than the enduring appeal of academic gossip. What is at stake are the rules of the game itself, i.e. the social conditions for the production of reliable knowledge and the associated persistence of a critical tradition.

Theory K wasn't just a bad book. Bad books come and go, and no doubt the universities produce rather more than their fair share. Inasmuch as it sought to change the rules of the academic game, *Theory K* was a bad *idea*. Therein lies its specifically academic interest and significance. In an institution whose historic *raison d'être* is ideas it quickly became the subject of gossip too scurrilous to repeat, but publicly it was either celebrated or greeted with silence. As such it came close to signalling a loss of institutional mana. One effect was that A. J. P. Taylor's suggestion (during the 1960s) that 'the universities are finishing schools for the middle classes and should be subsidised by the publishers of *Vogue*', came to seem much more acerbic and much less whimsical than when he made it.

But learning how to sip sherry without getting your bottom lip wet is not a justification for the autonomy which academics still enjoy. The warrant for that autonomy is what it always was—namely, that it is socially conducive to the production of good ideas and politically necessary for the criticism of bad ones. If that social mandate is to be honoured in more than a purely formal sense, the ideas in question must also matter beyond the confines of the university itself. But the choice is not between the university as an ivory tower on the one hand or the university as a service station on the other; between an institution wholly insulated from the wider society and one which is wholly subordinated to it; between, if you will, the not-at-all benign neglect of television, and an altogether-too-benign genuflection towards not-so-benign business interests. It is instead about finding ways to reconcile the full complexity and difficulty of those ideas which are legitimately the academic stock in trade, with a responsiveness to the society which supports their elaboration. In brief, how, in this time and in this place, can 'democratic' and 'intellect' be made to move into fruitful combinations with each other?

The answers to that question invite another volume, for we can expect the responses to be as plural as their determinations. Nevertheless, a brief record of just one such achievement provides an appropriate conclusion to this book. Appropriate in that the book can end as it began— with a probing of the relation between youth culture and formal education, as it emerges from the intersection between our daughters' evolving cultural preferences and the extant cultural resources of the secondary-school system. For our elder daughter, two teachers of maths and physics have succeeded in forging a cultural link between their respective subject specialties and some of the aspirations, hopes and difficulties to which popular culture speaks.

It is just this kind of elective affinity which is evident in George Steiner's observation that 'there is an age factor which makes popular music more like modern mathematics and physics than the humanities . . . (in that) the young have a tension-span, a suppleness of appropriation denied to the old' (Steiner 1971, p.91). But beyond this is his acknowledgement that it is the language worlds of mathematical and symbolic notation which give expression to 'the commanding energy: in material fact, in the forward dreams which define us . . . To have some personal *rapport* with the sciences is, very probably, to be in contact with that which has most force of life and comeliness in our reduced condition' (Steiner 1971, p.98). It is by a strategy of prospecting for the continuity of individual genius amongst these 'languages outside the word' that Steiner determinedly keeps faith with that cultural tradition which he represents so sublimely. But there is in Steiner's magisterial and elegant prose a recognition that the sciences are distinguished from the humanities by 'their collectivity and inner calendar . . . Because it carries the past within it, language, unlike mathematics, draws backwards . . . to the place of necessary, beloved shadows. For the scientist, time and the light lie before' (Steiner 1971, p.102).

This may be altogether too rhetorical and overblown for most local tastes. Certainly the sixth-form classroom and the teachers that prompted such an oratorical aside are overtly more pragmatic, matter of fact and wary of sentimentality. But that those two teachers have worked together to create a culture of science within that classroom, and that that culture is experienced by their students as technically demanding but personally and socially rewarding, does nevertheless depend upon the kind of foundation to which Steiner refers. The combined course that they have developed is obliged to run the gauntlet of official inspection, but it is nevertheless constructed at a tangent to, and goes well beyond, the formally approved curriculum. It is a class in which everyone is at the very edge of their abilities, in which everyone is struggling but struggling together, extending themselves and others. One or two of its members are (to employ a telling adjective) forbiddingly bright, but all of them are, of course, smart; they have all already succeeded by the standards of the educational system. (If this story has a moral, it is *not* about the possibility of a general model, but rather about the general possibilities of customised models.) The class is less about official standards than about the opening up of a world; about creating a dominion of signs in and through which students can construct a measure of themselves that is both linked to a larger pattern of meaning, and played out in the course of interaction with their peers. That one of those teachers gives of his spare time in order to introduce youngsters to windsurfing, and that the other organises the school tramping club is at once consistent with such a cultural pattern, and with this country's traditional best dream of itself. Neither 'man alone' nor 'a scout troop with the wrong map' can provide the precedent for such taken-for-granted combinations of seriousness and pleasure, of modernity and continuity, of the popular and the difficult. It may now be too late to retrieve the meaning of 'excellent' from the damage done to it by the celebration of mediocrity. But if that meaning can be salvaged, then this classroom and its unsung, gifted and (only slightly) wayward teachers would qualify with honours.

1 Early printings had a more or less plain cover, but this was later displaced by one which featured photographs of four company headquarters. Of those four, three subsequently went into receivership.
2 In Radway's analysis this in turn is seen as working to reinforce the very structure (i.e. patriarchy) which makes such fantasies necessary.
3 In 1984 (*Business Week*) the doyen of management writers, Peter Drucker, declared (rather too uncharitably) that Peters and Waterman's was 'a book for juveniles'. There has, however, been a growing critical literature, restricted largely to specialist journals (e.g. Carroll 1983; Mitchell 1985; Johnson *et al.*, 1985; Hitt & Ireland 1987).
4 For the cynics, for the record—and with some hesitation: Yes, I am (by choice) a member of an Arts Faculty, but I taught in a business school for almost a decade (independently ranked in Britain's top three and Europe's top ten); my most recent academic paper appears in the oldest of the British management journals; and I am on the editorial board of the newest.

References

Adorno, Theodor & Max Horkheimer, 1979. 'Enlightenment as Mass Deception' in their *Dialectic of Enlightenment*, London, Verso (first published 1944).

Arlen, Michael, 1980. *Thirty Seconds*, New York, Farrar, Strauss & Giroux.

Anderson, Benedict, 1983. *Imagined Communities: Reflections on the Origin and Spread of Nationalism*, London, Verso.

Baker, Mary, 1979. *Immigrant Women*, Christchurch, Society for Research on Women.

Barthes, Roland, 1973. *Mythologies*, London, Paladin.

Barthes, Roland , 1975. *S/Z*, New York, Hill & Wang.

Barthes, Roland, 1977. *Roland Barthes by Roland Barthes*, New York, Hill & Wang.

Barthes, Roland , 1988. *The Semiotic Challenge*, New York, Hill & Wang.

Bertram, Jean, 1978. 'The Importance of Perception', *Islands*, 21, pp.220–3.

Bettelheim, Bruno, 1976. *The Uses of Enchantment*, London, Thames & Hudson.

Bloom, Allan, 1987. *The Closing of the American Mind*, New York, Simon & Schuster.

Bourdieu, Pierre, 1977. *Outline of a Theory of Practice*, London, Cambridge Univ. Press.

Bourdieu, Pierre, 1984. *Distinction: A Social Critique of the Judgement of Taste*, London, Routledge.

Brown, Mary Ellen, 1990. *Television and Women's Culture*, Sydney, Currency Press.

Buchanan, Kerry, 1984. 'Hip Hop to Be Bop', *AND/2*, pp.75–82.

Business Week, 1984. 'Who's Excellent Now?', 5 November, pp.46–55.

Calder, Alex, 1987. 'The Pleasures and Politics of Watching the Sandbaggers', Auckland University Winter Lecture Series.

Carroll, Lewis, 1971. *Alice's Adventures in Wonderland* and *Through the Looking Glass*, London, Oxford Univ. Press.

Carroll, D., 1983. 'A disappointing search for excellence', *Harvard Business Review*, Nov-Dec, pp.78–88.

Carter, Ian, 1990. *Ancient Cultures of Conceit*, London, Routledge.

Carter, Ian & Nick Perry, 1987. 'Rembrandt in Gumboots; Rural Imagery in New Zealand Television Advertisements', in Jock Phillips (ed.), *Te Whenua Te Iwi: The Land and the People*, Wellington, Allen & Unwin/Port Nicholson Press, pp.61-72.

Chapman, Robert, 1973. 'Fiction and the Social Pattern', in Wystan Curnow (ed.), *Essays in New Zealand Literature*, Auckland, Heinemann, pp.71–98.

Copland, R. A., 1973. 'The Goodly Roof', in Wystan Curnow (ed.), *Essays in New Zealand Literature*, Auckland, Heinemann, pp.43–53.

Crothers, Charles, 1983. 'Reflections on Barbed Wire and Riot Squads', *New Zealand Cultural Studies Working Group Journal*, no. 7.

Curnow, Allen & Ngaio Marsh, 1945. 'A Dialogue by Way of Introduction', *First Yearbook of the Arts in New Zealand*, Wellington, H. H. Tombs.

Curnow, Wystan, 1973. 'High Culture in a Small Province', in Wystan Curnow (ed.), *Essays in New Zealand Literature*, pp.155–71.

Davin, Dan, 1978. 'Three Encounters Thirty Years Ago', *Islands*, 21, pp.302–5.

De Jong, Piet, 1986. 'Making Sense of New Zealand Rugby', *Sites*, 12, pp.29–42.

During, Simon, 1983. 'Towards a Revision of Local Critical Habits', *AND/1*, pp.75–93.

Eco, Umberto, 1985. *Reflections on The Name of the Rose*, London, Secker & Warburg.

Eco, Umberto, 1987. *Travels in Hyperreality*, London, Picador.

Edelman, Murray, 1977. *Political Language*, New York, Academic Press.

Ellis, John, 1982. *Visible Fictions*, London, Routledge.

Empson, William, 1930. *Seven Types of Ambiguity*, London, Chatto & Windus.

Evans, Patrick, 1980. 'Paradise or Slaughterhouse: Aspects of New Zealand Proletarian Fiction', *Islands*, 28, pp.71–86.

Evans, Patrick, 1981.'David Ballantyne and the Art of Writing in New Zealand', *Islands*, 31–32, pp.30–40.

Ewen, Stewart, 1989. *All Consuming Passions*, New York, Basic Books.

Fairburn, A. R. D., 1944. *We New Zealanders*, Wellington, Progressive   Publishers.

Farnsworth, John, 1992. 'Mainstream or Minority: Ambiguities in State or Market Arrangements for New Zealand Television', in John Deeks & Nick Perry (eds.), *Controlling Interests*, Auckland, Auckland Univ. Press, pp.191–207.

Fiske, John, 1987. 'Miami Vice, Miami Pleasure', *Cultural Studies*, 1, pp.113-19.

Fiske, John, 1989a. *Understanding Popular Culture*, Boston, Unwin Hyman.

Fiske, John, 1989b. *Reading the Popular*, London & Boston, Unwin Hyman.

Fiske, John, Bob Hodge & Graeme Turner, 1987. *Myths of Oz: Reading Australian Popular Culture*, Sydney, Allen & Unwin.

Fougere, Geoff, 1981. 'The Shattered Mirror', *Comment*, Nov., pp.12–14.

Fougere, Geoff, 1989. 'Sport, Culture and Identity: The Case of Rugby Football', in David Novitz & W. E. Willmott (eds), *Culture and Identity in New Zealand*, Wellington, Government Print.

French, Phillip, 1977. 'Media Marlowes', in M. Gross (ed.), *The World of Raymond Chandler*, London, Weidenfeld & Nicolson.

Gamman, Lois & M. Marshment (eds.), 1988. *The Female Gaze*, London, Women's Press.

Gardiner D. & K. S. Walker (eds.), 1962. *Raymond Chandler Speaking*, London, Hamish Hamilton.

Geertz, Clifford, 1974. 'Deep Play: Notes on the Balinese Cockfight', in Clifford Geertz (ed.), *Myth, Symbol and Culture*, New York, Norton.

Gellner, Ernest, 1966. *Thought and Change*, London, Weidenfeld & Nicolson.

Gellner, Ernest, 1968. *Words and Things*, Harmondsworth, Penguin.

Geraets, John, 1984. '*Landfall* 1947-66: Foundation and a Supplement', *AND/3*, 1984, pp.98–110.

Gitlin, Todd, 1983. *Inside Prime Time*, New York, Pantheon Books.

Gooding, Bruce, 1987. *KZ7: Inside Stories of Fear and Loathing*, Auckland, Reed Methuen.

Grant, A. K., 1984. Review of *Conversations on a Train and Other Critical Writing*, *New Outlook*, 10, p.38.

Gray, Alison, 1983. *The Jones Men*, Wellington, Reed.

Hall, Stuart, *et al.*, 1976. 'The Unity of Current Affairs Television', *Working Papers in Cultural Studies*, no.9, Birmingham, Univ. of Birmingham C.C.C.S.

Hebdige, Dick, 1982. 'Towards a Cartography of Taste, 1935–1962' in B. Waites, T. Bennett & G. Martin (eds), *Popular Culture Past and Present*, London, Croom Helm, pp.194–218.

Hirsch E. D., 1987. *Cultural Literacy*, Boston, Houghton.

Hitt, M. & D. Ireland, 1987. 'Peters and Waterman Revisited: the unending quest for excellence', *Academy of Management Executive*, 1, pp.91–98.

Hodge, Bob & David Tripp, 1986. *Children and Television: A Semiotic Approach*, Cambridge, Polity Press.

Horrocks, Roger, 1984. 'No Theory Permitted on these Premises', *AND/2*, pp.119–37.

Horrocks, Roger, 1985. 'Creating a Feature Film Industry', *Journal of Popular Culture*, 19(2), pp.149–58.

Huyssen, Andreas, 1986. 'Mass Culture as Woman: Modernism's Other', in Tania Modleski (ed.), *Studies in Entertainment: Critical Approaches to Mass Culture*, Bloomington/Indianapolis, Indiana Univ. Press, pp.188–208.

Ihimaera, Witi, 1977. *The New Net Goes Fishing*, Auckland, Heinemann.

Inkson, Kerr, Brian Henshall, Nick Marsh, Gill Ellis, 1986. *Theory K*, Auckland, David Bateman.

James, Clive, 1977. *Visions Before Midnight*, London, Jonathan Cape.

James, Clive, 1982. *From the Land of Shadows*, London, Jonathan Cape.

Jarvie, Ian, 1964. *The Revolution in Anthropology*, London, Routledge.

Johnson, B., A. Natarajan, A. Rappaport, 1985. 'Shareholder Returns and Corporate Excellence', *Journal of Business Strategy*, Fall, pp.52–62.

Jones, Lawrence, 1981. 'The Inside Story: Helen Shaw, Russell Haley and the Other Tradition', *Islands*, 31–32, pp.120–35.

Jones, Lawrence, 1982. 'Ronald Hugh Morrieson and Post Provincial Fiction', *Landfall*, 144, pp. 461-471.

Jones, Lawrence, 1989. 'Versions of the Dream: Literature and the Search for Identity', in David Novitz & Bill Willmott (eds.), *Culture and Identity in New Zealand*, pp.187–211.

Joyce, James, 1956. *A Portrait of the Artist as a Young Man*, London, Jonathan Cape.

King, Michael, 1977. *Te Puea*, Auckland, Hodder & Stoughton.

King, Michael, 1985. *Being Pakeha*, Auckland, Hodder & Stoughton.

Kress, Gunter R., 1976. 'Structuralism and Popular Culture', in C. W. E. Bigsby (ed.), *Approaches to Popular Culture*, London, Edward Arnold.

Kuhn, Thomas, 1970. *The Structure of Scientific Revolutions*, 2nd ed., Chicago, Chicago Univ. Press.

Kumar, Krishan, 1975. 'Holding the Middle Ground', *Sociology*, 9, pp.67–88.

Lambert, Max (ed.), 1989. *Air New Zealand Almanac*, 5th ed., Wellington, New Zealand Press Association.

Lealand, Geoff, 1988. *A Foreign Egg in Our Nest? American Popular Culture in New Zealand*, Wellington, Victoria Univ. Press.

Legat, Nicola, 1986. 'Atareta Poananga and Te Ahi Kaa: Their Message for Pakeha', *Metro*, March, pp.44–58.

Machery, Pierre, 1978. *A Theory of Literary Production*, London, Routledge.

Macshane, Frank, 1976. *The Life of Raymond Chandler*, London, Jonathan Cape.

Mailer, Norman, 1957. 'The White Negro', reprinted in his *Advertisements for Myself* (1961), London, Andre Deutsch, pp.281–302.

Marcus, Greil, 1975. *Mystery Train: Images of America in Rock 'n' Roll Music*, New York, Dutton.

McCauley, Sue, 1982. *Other Halves*, Auckland, Hodder & Stoughton.

McCormick, E. H., 1959. *New Zealand Literature: A Survey*, London, Oxford Univ. Press.

McEldowney, Dennis, 1976. *Frank Sargeson in his Time*, Dunedin, John McIndoe.

McGregor, Douglas, 1960. *The Human Side of Enterprise*, New York, McGraw Hill.

McLauchlan, Gordon, 1976. *The Passionless People*, Auckland, Cassell.

McLuhan, Marshall, 1964. *Understanding Media*, New York, New American Library.

McNair Surveys Ltd, 1986. *Trans Tasman Attitudes Survey*, prepared for Australia & New Zealand Foundation.

Metro, 1986. '86 for 86', Jan., pp.77–88.

Metz, Christian, 1982. *Psychoanalysis and Cinema*, London, Macmillan.

Meurant, Ross, 1982. *The Red Squad Story*, Auckland, Harlen.

Mitchell, Austin, 1972. *The Half Gallon, Quarter Acre Pavlova Paradise*, Christchurch, Whitcombe & Tombs.

Mitchell, T., 1985. 'In Search of Excellence versus The 100 Best Companies to Work for in America: a question of perspectives and value', Academy of Management Review, 10, pp.350–5.

Modleski, Tania, 1982. Loving With a Vengeance: Mass Produced Fantasies for Women, New York, Methuen.

Morison, Elting E., 1962. 'Scientists in Decision Making', in M. Greenberger (ed.), Computers and the World of the Future, Cambridge, MIT Press.

Morley, David, 1986. Family Television, London, Comedia.

Morris, Meaghan, 1990. 'Banality in Cultural Studies' in Patricia Mellencamp (ed.), The Logics of Television, Bloomington, Indiana Univ. Press, pp.14–43.

Mullins, Pat, 1981a. 'Theoretical Perspectives on Australian Urbanisation: I', Australian and New Zealand Journal of Sociology, 17(1), pp.65–76.

Mullins, Pat, 1981b. 'Theoretical Perspectives on Australian Urbanisation: II', Australian and New Zealand Journal of Sociology, 17(3), pp.35–43.

Mulvey, Laura, 1975. 'Visual Pleasure and Narrative Cinema', Screen, 16(3), pp.6–18.

Murdoch, Iris, 1954. Under The Net, London, Chatto & Windus.

NZ Dept of Statistics, 1989. New Zealand Official Year Book 1988–89, Wellington, Dept of Statistics.

OECD, 1975. Economic Survey: Japan, Paris, OECD.

OECD, 1990. Economic Survey: Japan, Paris, OECD.

Ollsen, E. A., 1962. 'The Conditions of Culture', in Charles Brasch (ed.), Landfall Country, Christchurch, Caxton.

Openshaw, Roger & Roy Shuker, 1988. 'Silent Movies and Comics', in M. McKinnon (ed.), The American Connection, Wellington, Allen & Unwin, pp.52-65.

Orwell, George, 1957. 'Raffles and Miss Blandish', in Bernard Rosenberg & David M. White (eds), Mass Culture, New York, Free Press.

Ouchi, William, 1981. Theory Z: how American business can meet the Japanese challenge, Reading, Addison-Wesley.

Parkin, Rosa & Charley Parkin, 1974. 'Peter Rabbit and the Grundrisse', European Journal of Sociology, 15, pp.181–3.

Pasternak, Boris, 1958. Dr Zhivago, London, Collins/Harvill.

Pearson, Bill, 1962. 'Fretful Sleepers' in C. Brasch (ed.), Landfall Country.

Pearson, Bill, 1974. 'The Maori in Literature', in his Fretful Sleepers and Other Essays, Auckland, Heinemann.

Penman, Ian, 1986. 'The Plot Chickens', The Face, 70, Feb.

Perry, Nick, 1977. 'A Comparative Analysis of Paradigm Proliferation', British Journal of Sociology, 28, pp.38–50.

Perry, Nick, 1984. 'Catch, Class and Bureaucracy: The Meaning of Joseph Heller's Catch 22', Sociological Review, 32, pp.719–42.

Perry, Nick, 1990. 'Review Essay: Frankfurters, French Fries and a Spaghetti Sandwich', Landfall, 173, pp.88–92.

Perry, Nick, 1992a. 'Upside Down or Downside Up? Sectoral Interests, Structural Change and Public Policy', in John Deeks & Nick Perry (eds), *Controlling Interests: Business, Society and the State in New Zealand*, Auckland, Auckland Univ. Press, pp.36–58.

Perry, Nick, 1992b. 'Conclusion: On Policing a Dozen Cases of Disorderly Conduct', in John Deeks & Nick Perry (eds), *Controlling Interests*, Auckland, Auckland Univ. Press, pp.230–40.

Perry, Nick, 1993. 'The Peculiarities of English', *History of the Human Sciences*, 6, pp.91–100.

Perry, Nick & Roy Wilkie, 1975. 'J.G. Ballard and the New Science Fiction', *Question*, 9, pp.38–49.

Peters, Tom & Robert Waterman, 1982. *In Search of Excellence*, New York, Harper & Row.

Phillips, Jock, 1987. *A Man's Country?*, Auckland, Penguin.

Poincaré, Henri, 1958. *The Value of Science*, New York, Dover.

Poole, Michael, 1984. 'The Cult of the Generalist—British Television Criticism 1936–1983', *Screen*, 25(2).

Poster, Mark, 1990. *The Mode of Information*, Cambridge, Polity Press.

Pound, Ezra, 1952. *The Spirit of Romance*, London, Peter Owen.

Radway, Janice, 1984. *Reading the Romance: Women, Patriarchy and Popular Literature*, Durham, Univ. of North Carolina Press.

Rambali, Paul, 1985. 'Towards the Matt Black Dream Home', *The Face*, 67, pp.48–51.

Rhodes, H. Winston, 1969. *Frank Sargeson*, New York, Twayne.

Rich, Adrienne, 1983. 'Split at the Root', in Ursula Owens (ed.), *Fathers: Reflections by Daughters*, London, Virago Press, pp.170–86.

Richter, David, 1974. *Fables End*, Chicago, Chicago Univ. Press.

Ritchie, James, 1985. 'Writer Alone', *Listener*, 14 Dec., pp.60–61.

Root, Jane, 1986. *Open the Box*, London, Comedia.

Rose, Margaret, 1978. *Reading The Young Marx and Engels*, London, Croom Helm.

Ryle, Gilbert, 1964. *Dilemmas*, London, Cambridge Univ. Press.

Sapir, Edward, 1921. *Language: An Introduction to the Study of Speech*, New York, Harcourt Brace.

Sargeson, Frank, 1965. 'Beginnings', *Landfall*, 74, pp.122–9.

Shadbolt, Maurice, 1980. *The Lovelock Version*, London, Hodder & Stoughton.

Silverman, David & Brian Torode, 1980. *The Material Word*, London, Routledge.

Silverstone, Roger, 1981. *The Message of Television*, London, Heinemann.

Sinclair, Keith, 1959. *The History of New Zealand*, Harmondsworth, Penguin.

Sinclair, Keith, 1976. *Walter Nash*, Auckland, Auckland Univ. Press/Oxford Univ. Press.

Sinclair, Keith, 1983. *A History of the University of Auckland, 1883-1983*, Auckland, Auckland Univ. Press/Oxford Univ. Press.

Smith, Barry & David Thorns, 1980. 'Housing Markets and Submarkets: An

Analysis of the Role of Financial Institutions in the Allocation of Housing', *Australian and New Zealand Journal of Sociology*, 16(1), pp.4–13.

Sontag, Susan, 1966. 'Notes on Camp', in her *Against Interpretation*, New York, Farrar, Strauss & Giroux.

Stead, C. K., 1981. *In the Glass Case*, Auckland, Auckland Univ. Press/Oxford Univ. Press.

Steiner, George, 1971. *In Bluebeard's Castle*, London, Faber & Faber.

Steiner, George, 1978. *On Difficulty and Other Essays*, New York, Oxford Univ. Press.

Thompson, E. P., 1968. *The Making of the English Working Class*, Harmondsworth, Penguin.

Trilling, Lionel, 1950. *The Liberal Imagination*, New York, Viking.

Trussell, Denys, 1984. *Fairburn*, Auckland, Auckland Univ. Press/Oxford Univ. Press.

Warshow, Robert, 1961. *The Immediate Experience*, New York, Doubleday.

Watson, James, & A. Hill, 1984. *A Dictionary of Communication and Media Studies*, London, Edward Arnold.

White, Helen, 1985. 'Foreskin in 1985', *Landfall*, 156, pp.490–2.

Williams, Raymond, 1960. *The Long Revolution*, London, Chatto & Windus.

Williams, Raymond, 1973. *The Country and the City*, London, Chatto & Windus.

Williams, Raymond, 1974. *Television: Technology and Cultural Form*, London, Fontana.

Wolfe, Tom, 1965. *The Kandy-Kolored Tangerine-Flake Streamline Baby*, London, Mayflower Books.

Wood, Brennon, 1984. *Smashing the Audience*, Palmerston North, Dept of Sociology, Massey Univ.

Worsley, Peter, 1957. *The Trumpet Shall Sound*, London, MacGibbon & Kee.

Index